Exceptional Monologues for Men and Women

Volume 1

Edited by Roxane Heinze-Bradshaw
and Katherine DiSavino

A SAMUEL FRENCH ACTING EDITION

SAMUEL
FRENCH
FOUNDED 1830

NEW YORK HOLLYWOOD LONDON TORONTO

SAMUELFRENCH.COM

ACKNOWLEDGEMENTS

We would like to thank Amy Rose Marsh, Ken Dingledine, Shari Perkins, and Emma Halpern, who were all instrumental in the creation and development of this project.

Keep an eye out for the Volume 2, as well as a scene book from Samuel French, available Summer 2010!

A NOTE FROM THE EDITORS

Welcome to the inaugural edition of **Exceptional Monologues for Men and Women, Volume 1**! We are very pleased to be able to present you with these wonderful monologues, written by some of the most exciting writers on the scene today, including Adam Bock, Sarah Ruhl, and Ken Ludwig, just to name a few. We think you'll be able to find excellent audition and class material within these pages, as well as a window into many of the new titles that we publish. We've divided the book into Male and Female, and then from there into Comedic and Dramatic. Of course, such black and white categorizations don't always convey the complexities of a given monologue or play, but we've tried to gauge the overall mood of the chosen monologue in particular, independent of the play in which it appears. So be sure to look at the play synopsis provided to gain a better sense of the play as a whole. In addition to a play synopsis, each monologue is provided with a scene synopsis, in order to help you contextualize the given selection and get into the character's head. Have some thoughts about the character's motivation? Why not jot them down in the notes section provided for your convenience with every piece. Also, if you flip to the back of the book, we've provided a thematic index as yet another tool in your search for the perfect-for-you monologue.

We've also placed the monologues in ascending order of age range within each section, for ease of use. But don't let that stop you from browsing others! There is a maximum of two monologues from each play included, so if a certain piece strikes your fancy, why not order the full script and look for more material? We've provided complete play descriptions in a play glossary at the back of the book and/or you can check our website for more information (samuelfrench.com) before taking the plunge and purchasing the whole work. We certainly do hope that this monologue collection might entice you to expand your theatrical horizons and explore the multifaceted world of contemporary playwriting. We think you will find it just as exciting as we do!

Break a leg!

Roxane Heinze-Bradshaw, Editor &
Katherine DiSavino, Assistant Editor

CONTENTS

MALE COMEDIC MONOLOGUES

FEMALE COMEDIC MONOLOGUES

MALE DRAMATIC MONOLOGUES

FEMALE DRAMATIC MONOLOGUES

COMEDIC MONOLOGUES

MALE

From Up Here
Liz Flahive

Play Synopsis: Kenny Barrett did something that has everyone worried. He wishes he could just make it through the rest of his senior year unnoticed, but that's going to be hard since he has to publicly apologize to his entire high school. At home, his mother is struggling with a rocky start to her second marriage and a surprise visit from her estranged sister. A play about a family limping out the door in the morning and coming home no matter what.

Character: Charlie
Age: Teens
Genre: Comedic

Scene Synopsis: Charlie – an incessant talker with a musical soul – has a big crush on Lauren. He ropes Kenny into being his backup singer for a new song he wrote, and then decides to spill his guts to a slightly mortified Lauren.

Notes:

THEMES: DATING, NERVES, HOPE

From Up Here

CHARLIE. You know, I wrote you that song. I wrote it because when I see you, normally, it's just, it's just a mess. When I think about you I can't breathe and I look at you and I'm not sure you're real. You just look like...Like if someone were to say, Hey can you draw a girl and I drew you they'd be like, hey, that's a perfect drawing of a girl, you're a real good artist. And my hands get all shaky when I want to touch you and you know that great hollow feeling you get in your stomach when you see someone you've been thinking about for days and then you turn the corner and there they are. And it's like... *(He exhales all the air in his lungs until the breath just stops.)* And the bottom drops out and I feel like I have no actual mass or dimension and it's like maybe I'm seeing you at that moment after having thought about you because you were, at the same time, thinking about me. And that's how we ended up at the exact same place in the exact same moment. By thinking about it that much. Do you need a ride?

THEMES: Dating, Nerves, Hope

Collective Dating: Natural Dating
VB Leghorn

Play Synopsis: *Collective Dating* is a wacky collection of romantic comedies based on the world of dating. In "Natural Dating," Sara learns a little of patience and love from George, a peaceful admirer of butterflies. Compared to her thuggish suitor, George with his passive demeanor seems like a knight in…nude armor.

Character: George
Age: 20s – 30s
Genre: Comedic

Scene Synopsis: In a nudist colony where members of the collective like to observe butterflies, George explains to Sara why he only watches these creatures and in doing so, touches on the nature of other things as well.

Notes:

Collective Dating: Natural Dating

GEORGE. No! I'm here to observe butterflies, not capture them. Imagine, flying around, minding your own business when some huge net is thrown over you, trapping your wings. You struggle, trying to wriggle free, but it's no use.

Sticky, sweaty hands grab you by the wings, rubbing off the magic fairy dust that makes you fly. Your legs are bound and slowly you die of starvation or perhaps you just give up in despair knowing that you will never take flight again.

And that's not the worst of it. Once you're dead, you're stuck through the gut with a pin onto a piece of wood, You don't do that, do you?

Messiah On the Frigidaire
John Culbertson

Play Synopsis: The small town of Elroy, South Carolina is thrust into the evangelical spotlight when what seems to be the image of Jesus appears on a refrigerator in a trailer park. The discovery sets into motion a frenzy of conflict, communion and good old fashioned commerce. When the National Investigator turns the appearance into front-page headlines, their trailer park becomes a Mecca for miracle seekers, soul searchers and disciples with a decidedly political agenda.

Character: Dwayne
Age: 20s – 30s
Genre: Comedic

Scene Synopsis: After the image of Jesus appears in their trailer park, Dwayne shares his unique view of evolution, faith and miracles with his wife, Lou Ann.

Notes:

Messiah On the Frigidaire

DWAYNE. I guess it started when I realized there were some major problems with evolution. I know you don't believe in evolution, but just shut up and let me finish. I just couldn't figure out why some monkeys would evolve into humans, and others would just stay monkeys. You follow me?

I just don't think monkeys would look around and say, "Hey, that guy used to be a monkey, and now he's makin' weapons outta brass. I suppose I should evolve too…Naah, I'll just sit here and eat bananas." I mean once humans started evolving, we all evolved. You don't have a bunch of cavemen still walkin' around today. You see, somethin' happened to a couple of those monkeys, and I know what it was. Aliens.

You see, I figure there was this race of super aliens travelin' around the universe. You know, just lookin' around. Well, they landed on earth, and I'm not sure if it was some kind of experiment, or whether they were just real lonely after all them miles on a space ship, but either way, they impregnated the monkeys. You see, that explains why ALL the monkeys didn't evolve. They didn't fool around with the aliens….those super

Okay…You see, a couple a thousand years ago the aliens cameback. Yeah, but no monkeys this time…this time they impregnated just one person. Mary. You know what it says about that angel appearin' in her room and tellin' her not to be afraid and gettin' her all pregnant and everything? That was an alien. Jesus was human too, but he got a double dose of those super alien genes, and that's why he was so wise and everything. He was way beyond us in mental things, physical, too. All those miracles? He was just usin' his alien powers.

Bach at Leipzig
Itamar Moses

Play Synopsis: Leipzig, Germany – 1722. Johann Kuhnau, revered organist of the Thomaskirche, suddenly dies, leaving his post vacant. The town council invites musicians to audition for the coveted position, among them young Johann Sebastian Bach. In an age where musicians depend on patronage from the nobility or the church to pursue their craft, the post at a prominent church in a cultured city is a near guarantee of fame and fortune which is why some of the candidates are willing to resort to any lengths to secure it.

Character: Lenck
Age: 30s
Genre: Comedic

Scene Synopsis: An eager organist arrives in Leipzig and recounts his trip, his excitement and his plan to ensure he gets the job in a letter to his love from home.

Notes:

Bach at Leipzig

LENCK. Leipzig. June, 1722.

My dear Catherina:

I have arrived safely, and in time, having arranged passage with a gentleman who allowed me to accompany his carriage. Because he did not know I was there. Clinging to the underside of it. As I am fond of saying: I, Georg Lenck, am so poor that I cannot afford even a middle name with which to distinguish myself from other Georgs. But that, after all, is why I've come. For this memorial is to be hosted by the Leipzig Council itself, the very men charged with selecting Kuhnau's replacement. Here I will reverse my fortunes at last.

I have promised this before, it's true. As when I had you defraud your parents by feigning an expensive illness called Bogus Fever. I apologize again for discounting your warnings regarding your father's familiarity with medicine. But, after all, you were feverish. In any case, here is a chance for real glory: a post in Leipzig! *(Beat.)* I have promised that I could win a post in Leipzig before, it's true. When I auditioned at a church surrounded by cobblers, and, for some reason, under a bridge. But I faced a rival who was insurmountable. Once he blackmailed me with my history of feigning expensive illnesses.

This time I have left no room for error. I come bearing dozens of letters in praise of my musical talent. And, thanks to my adept calligraphy, each is in a different script! And each signed by an entirely fictitious Duke!

This is indeed a happy day.

Getting Sara Married
Sam Bobrick

Play Synopsis: Sara Hastings is an unmarried lawyer in her mid-thirties. Her Aunt Martha has decided to find Sara a husband by having the prospective groom bopped over the head and brought to Sara's apartment. Aunt Martha's choice is Brandon Cates, a young man who is already engaged to be married. After a number of mishaps and confrontations, Brandon comes to realize that Sara is really the girl for him.

Character: Brandon
Age: 30s
Genre: Comedic

Scene Synopsis: Brandon explains to Sara how he has been preparing himself for married life – by visualizing how bad it will be. After describing how he pictures newlywed life, he goes on to depict what it will be like when he and his fiancee have a child and have to move out of Manhattan and into the suburbs.

Notes:

THEMES: COMMITMENT, CONTROL, MARRIAGE

Getting Sara Married

BRANDON. So now I have to give up my nice, wonderful, hip New York apartment and move out to the suburbs, a million miles away, from my favorite restaurants, my terrific gym, the young girl at Starbucks who pours my coffee every morning, the excitement, the pace, the energy of the city I truly love.

Along the way she makes me get rid of my great little sports car that I used to drive up to the Hamptons on summer weekends before I was married. I am now forced to own one of those stupid clunky SUV's which soon fills up with the same baby crap my wonderful little New York apartment was filled with. In no time at all, every inch of upholstery is covered with crusted slobber and sticky kiddy goo. In fact, from now on, everything I touch seems covered with crusted slobber and sticky kiddy goo.

As the kids get bigger my space grows smaller. Now there are bicycles and wagons and scooters and skate boards and bunk beds and drum sets and car pools and Little League and soccer practice, and every day it takes a little bit longer to drive up and back to work because every day there's more cars on the highway because every day there's more guys like me getting married and I'm always rushing and always late and now we have six kids and life becomes more hectic and jammed and cramped and I suddenly realize I haven't seen my wife naked in fifteen years because three of our six kids are still sleeping in our bedroom. Besides, my wife has no time for sex because she's busy twenty four hours a day figuring out how to put more of her stuff in my closet space.

THEMES: COMMITMENT, CONTROL, MARRIAGE

A Fish Story

Jon Tuttle

Play Synopsis: George shoots a schnauzer and brings it triumphantly back to Zee, who stuffs his pillowcase with bloody fish parts. Fighting ensues, and the flood water outside is rising. For some reason, teenager daughter Annie dreams of escape from all this. Into their mountain cabin stumbles poor Frank, the perfect replacement for the son they lost. Now if only they can keep him without killing him, too.

Character: George
Age: 30s
Genre: Comedic

Scene Synopsis: After Frank shares a lofty opinion of a fish's ability to have "Death Perception," George decides to put him straight with his own version of what the life (and death) of a Fish is really like.

Notes:

A Fish Story

GEORGE. I'm gonna do you a favor here, Cochise. I'm gonna put this whole fish thing in proper perspective for you here. You watch this. You ready? This is The Life of a Fish.

I'm a fish. Here I am, swimmin' around and swimmin' around. Gee, I wonder where the hell I'm goin'? I can't tell, 'cause I got eyes on the sides of my head. There's only right here, right now. No need for memory, no need for worry. When I get where I'm goin', wherever that is, I'll forget where I just was, 'cause I'll be someplace else, which is as good as any other, as far as I can see, which ain't very, 'cause I got eyes on the sides of my head! Whoa! Look out for that dyke! Watch where you're goin'! – That's a fish joke. Think I'll relieve myself now. *(Fart sounds, with bubbles.)* Wonder where that went. No way a' knowin'! Think I'll have a few babies now – say, thirty-two. *(Birth sounds.)* Ah! There! All that work makes me hungry. Think I'll eat the fat ones. Nobody wants fat kids. *(He gobbles.)* Thanks, kids! Adios! Watch for sharks! – Another fish joke. Hell, where am I now? What difference does it make? None whatsoever. Wait! There's a bit nasty steel hook dressed up as an insect. Didn't one a' them rip out my gums last week? How would I know? Let's have lunch! I haven't eaten anything since beats me. Mmm! Tastes like nothing I recall! Wait a minute. Whoa! It's fighting back! Where am I going? Who the hell knows? Where have I been? I don't remember! *(He flops on the floor for a few seconds, then stops.)* Well, this is interesting. Got one eye on the sky, the other in the mud. Well, enough of this. I'll just swim away. *(He flops some more.)* Whew! Musta swum for miles. Whatever that means. Wait! There's a hairy legged fella, wearin' a dress! Maybe he knows where I am! Maybe I'll ask him. Ask him what? I don't remember! I don't remember I don't remem I don't. *(And he 'dies,' with his tongue hanging out.)*

THEMES: **DEATH, INTELLIGENCE, SURVIVAL**

Half and Half
James Sherman

Play Synopsis: In *Half and Half* two marriages, past and present, are explored in two related one-act plays. In the first act, set at a breakfast in 1970, the breadwinner husband reads the newspaper and the homemaker wife fries the eggs. In the present-day second act, the career-minded wife reads the paper and the stay-at-home husband cooks the frittata. With his unique comic insight, Sherman looks at how husbands and wives accept and reject their roles, how their roles have changed and, how their roles just might be changing back.

Character: Jeremy
Age: 30s
Genre: Comedic

Scene Synopsis: Jeremy discusses gender stereotyping, work, life and love with his wife, as he tries to help her understand that nothing is black and white, and many things can change with time.

Notes:

Half and Half

JEREMY. You know what? Don't give my mother all the credit. Just because I was a nice Jewish boy doesn't mean I couldn't be an asshole. I used to treat women like sex objects... Remember the Sexual Revolution? The minute I heard about the Sexual Revolution, I went out to enlist. Everybody thought it was about "peace" and "love," but I knew what it was really about. It was an excuse to get a lot of sex, no questions asked.

Then 1972, I'm at I.S.U. I see Marlo Thomas campaigning for Shirley Chisholm for president and I had such hots for Marlo Thomas... But who got Marlo Thomas?

Phil Donahue. There was Phil Donahue. And Alan Alda. And I saw it was good to be a nice guy. And it wasn't easy. I went back and forth. "I'm a nice guy. I'm an asshole. I'm a nice guy. I'm an asshole." Like Faye Dunaway in "China-town." "She's my sister. She's my daughter. She's my sister. She's my daughter." So I went to sensitivity training and encounter groups. I read Betty Friedan and Germaine Greer and Carol Gilligan. I raised my own damn consciousness. And then 1979.

"Kramer vs. Kramer." I saw "Kramer vs. Kramer" fourteen times. Like it was a training film. And I got it. Men can be the nurturers. We can get off the fast track.

So I quit my job at Leo Burnett and wrote my first novel about – Hey! – An asshole who becomes a sensitive guy. I was right there along with Mr. Mom and Mrs. Doubtfire and Three Men and a Baby. And I thought, "Great. This is it. This is the way it's going to be. You bring home the bacon and I'll make the quiche."... So don't say, "all men are jerks." It pisses me off. I achieved "sensitive guy-dom" through hard work and determination. I am a husband and father totally different from the way my father was a husband and father. And what do I get for it? You'll find me in the Museum of Pop Culture. Next to pet rocks and Leisure suits.

THEMES: LOVE, SEX, MARRIAGE

A Night at the Nutcracker
Billy Van Zandt and Jane Milmore

Play Synopsis: Reminiscent of the screwball farces during the golden age of cinema, this romping musical teams Felix T. Filibuster, the greatest detective in the world, up with Pinchie the silent butler, and his Italian friend and coworker, Pepponi. The trio tries to prove that Clyde Ratchette is trying to swindle the wealthy Mrs. Stuffington, who has just invested a bundle in the production of The Nutcracker Suite.

Character: Felix
Age: 30s
Genre: Comedic

Scene Synopsis: Mrs. Stuffington's son reveals to Felix that someone has taken all of the family jewels out of their safe. Convinced that Mr. Ratchette is behind it all and trying to swindle Mrs. Stuffington through their courtship, Felix tries to woo the rich woman away from the villain in his own, unique way.

Notes:

THEMES: LOVE, TRICKERY, FLIRTING

A Night at the Nutcracker

FELIX. Don't you see what I'm trying to tell you? Ratchette's all wrong for you. Give that heel the boot and let me take you away from all this. I can't help it. All us Filibusters are a little forward. Except for my cousin who was a little backward. And of course my uncle who had a little something going on the side. Don't you see what I'm saying? I love you. There I said it. It's love at first sight. And luckily for you, I've got glaucoma. You're the kind of girl I've been searching for my entire life. I never knew someone like you existed. In fact, this is exactly like finding Sasquatch. Or maybe it's just your Big Foot that makes me say that. Yeti it seems to be true. Oh, Connie. What can Ratchette give you that I can't, besides a bad toupee? And ugly children with bad toupees? Let me pull the rug out from under him… and him out from under his rug… Then it'll just be us. You and me. And me and you. And you and me. Just the six of us. We could make some beautiful music together. Me on the cello. You on the tuba. We could even travel the world. Paris, Rome, Paris.

I left my bag there – we had to go back!

Then it's off to Russia where we spend a vulgar night on the river. I mean, a night on the river Volga. Just you and me and those two big boats of yours. We make love in one of the boats, while I drink champagne out of your OTHER shoe. And there you are, the moonlight on your face. Yes, you and the moon. I can tell the difference because you've got bigger craters.

Eurydice
Sarah Ruhl

Play Synopsis: In *Eurydice,* Sarah Ruhl reimagines the classic myth of Orpheus through the eyes of its heroine. Dying too young on her wedding day, Eurydice must journey to the underworld, where she reunites with her father and struggles to remember her lost love. With contemporary characters, ingenious plot twists, and breathtaking visual effects, the play is a fresh look at a timeless love story.

Character: Father
Age: 30s – 40s
Genre: Comedic

Scene Synopsis: Upon entering the underworld, people are dipped in a River of Forgetfulness. However, Eurydice's father, part of the underworld, has not forgotten everything like the other souls around him. On his daughter's wedding day, he writes a letter to her, longing to be with her and knowing his words might never reach her in the world above.

Notes:

THEMES: LOVE, FAMILY, MARRIAGE

Eurydice

FATHER. Dear Eurydice,

A letter for you on your wedding day.

There is no choice of any importance in life but the choosing of a beloved. I haven't met Orpheus, but he seems like a serious young man. I understand he's a musician.

(The father thinks – oh, dear.)

If I were to give a speech at your wedding I would start with one or two funny jokes and then I might offer some words of advice. I would say:

Cultivate the arts of dancing and small talk.

Everything in moderation.

Court the companionship and respect of dogs.

Grilling a fish or toasting bread without burning requires singleness of purpose, vigilance and steadfast watching.

Keep quiet about politics, but vote for the right man.

Take care to change the light bulbs.
Continue to give yourself to others because that's the ultimate satisfaction in life–to love, accept, honor and help others.

As for me, this is what it's like being dead: The atmosphere smells. And there are strange high pitched noises–like a tea kettle always boiling over. But it doesn't seem to bother anyone. And, for the most part, there is a pleasant atmosphere and you can work and socialize, much like at home. I'm working in the business world and it seems that, here, you can better see the far reaching consequences of your actions.

Also, I am one of the few dead people who still remembers how to read and write. That's a secret. If anyone finds out, they might dip me in the River again.

I write you letters. I don't know how to get them to you.

Love,

Your father.

THEMES: LOVE, FAMILY, MARRIAGE

Who Killed the Sausage King
Roger Karshner

Play Synopsis: The police are baffled after Wilbur Smith, "The Sausage King," is strangled with a roll of his own sausage. After several months, the authorities, unable to unscramble the dilemma, call in the services of Farlow Cranston, ace private investigator and renowned solver of arcane cases. Cranston, with unflappable grandiloquence and fractured logic, unravels the mystery via a farcical route that leads to its conclusion. Expect the unexpected in this delightful melange.

Character: Farlow Cranston
Age: 40s
Genre: Comedic

Scene Synopsis: Farlow reminisces with his assistant about an old case and his detective prowess, illustrated by how beautifully he solved everything in the end.

Notes:

Who Killed the Sausage King

FARLOW CRANSTON. *(He stands and paces grandly.)* Do you remember the Pangborn case? Clayton Pangborn, the famous writer. I recall arriving on the scene at three in the morning. It was an inclement night and required me wearing two trench coats. *(Expansive, pompous.)* It was a bloody mess, I'll tell you a naked corpse hanging upside down from a chandelier. I was immediately suspicious. We cut down the body and laid it on the floor. The forensic people went over the scene with a fine tooth comb and found nothing. I, however, deduced immediately that it had to be an inside job; someone who knew the chandelier was strong enough to hold a person. That was my first thought before the M.E. arrived, but upon close inspection of the body she found two small puncture holes in its neck. Dracula? Nonsense. No, it was obviously the work of an insidious fiend, someone who would resort to bizarre tactics to throw the authorities off the scent, and someone who was strong enough to hoist the body. So I turned my attention to the staff. I called them into the study. The housekeeper was a scrawny asthmatic that would have difficulty lifting her feather duster, so she was immediately dismissed. The gardener was an Octogenarian with a clubfoot. The victim's private secretary, however, was a strapping fellow with the temperament of a wolverine, who developed a pronounced twitch under my interrogation. Suspecting a clerical murder, I investigated the victim's desk and found a staple remover with traces of blood. When confronted with this, the man broke down and confessed. Profusely. It came to light that the fellow had been the victim's personal secretary for years and was responsible for correcting his sloppy manuscripts. He'd finally cracked under the pressure of removing faulty syntax. At trial, I recommended leniency on the grounds of literary insanity. He's currently serving twenty years and is the editor of the prison newsletter.

THEMES: CONSPIRACY, DEATH, WORK

The Iliad, The Odyssey and all of Greek Mythology in 99 Minutes or Less

Jay Hopkins and John Hunter

Play Synopsis: On a simple stage, with the clock ticking in front of everyone's eyes, the cast speeds through all of Greek Mythology. All the silly decisions, the absurd destinies, and the goofy characters are presented lightning-bolt fast with hysterical results as the clock is stopped with only seconds to spare.

Character: Zeus
Age: 40s – 50s
Genre: Comedic

Scene Synopsis: After being tricked by Prometheus, Zeus lays out his punishment and decides to dish out the ultimate revenge to Man – Woman!

Notes:

THEMES: POWER, PUNISHMENT, REVENGE

The Iliad, The Odyssey and all of Greek Mythology in 99 Minutes or Less

ZEUS. Argh!!! Prometheus!!! You tricked me! You are in big trouble mister. However, I've given my word and I'll stick to it. Prometheus! You did a bang up job with man, so I'm going to give you a brand new home up high on the Caucasus, a high jagged rock where you shall be bound by adamantine chains that none can break. And an eagle will come to visit you, and feast on your liver every day. All because...You pissed me off! And Man! Before I go, I want to give you a little gift from all the Gods, in fact that is her name, meaning "the gift of all." You pronounce it Pandora.

Oh YES! Man shall have his mate. She is of the same material and equal in most ways. She is brave and careless; angry and gracious; foolish and smarter than man by just a hair. Oh, and curious! So curious! She hungers for knowledge and will ask man questions. LOTS AND LOTS of questions. And when a man has all he needs, for he is simple and needs only food, sleep and a mate, she will wonder why? Why is that all he needs? Why doesn't he need more? Why doesn't he want more? If he had more, would he want it? Would he not want it? Why would he want it or not want it? Why? Why? Oh, I almost forgot. A present for Pandora.

Pandora, go and live with man. Be happy, have fun. Here is a gift for you. The only thing is you can NEVER open this box. Here's the key. Remember NEVER open the box. Now get out of here you crazy kids!

THEMES: POWER, PUNISHMENT, REVENGE

COMEDIC MONOLOGUES

FEMALE

Sunken Living Room
David Caudle

Play Synopsis: November, 1978. Wade Minnick, 16, is a slender, effeminate bookworm in suburban Miami. With his distracted mother out playing Bridge, and his pilot father away on a trip, his volatile brother Chip, 17, takes off on a dubious errand, leaving Wade alone with Chip's foxy pothead girlfriend. "Freak" Tammy teaches "brain" Wade more about life and about himself than he could learn from a dozen novels.

Character: Tammy
Age: Teens
Genre: Comedic

Scene Synopsis: Tammy explores the definitions of social circles, trying to figure out where to place Wade, her boyfriend's younger brother. She begins to toy with the idea of breaking these confines.

Notes:

Sunken Living Room

TAMMY. No, I'm a freak. Because I smoke pot and have sex and skip school. There's one freak in student government, but she's really a brain, who's just a drug addict with mental problems. Mostly freaks don't go in for student government. I think some of the brains have sex, too, and drink a little beer sometimes but they're in a lot of clubs and student government. The rednecks drink beer and have sex and skip school, but some of them are in student government. The jocks drink beer, smoke pot and have sex and skip school, but still some of them are in student government.

> *(Beat.)*

That's what Chip is. A freak-jock. If he didn't have black friends he'd be a freak-jock-redneck, 'cuz he's also friends with some of them, and I know he's bagged a few of the brain chicks, so actually you could say he's a freak-jock-redneck-brain, pretty much just across-the-board kinda guy.

> *(Beat.)*

Except he's not in student government.

> *(Beat.)*

Me, I'm just a freak. And you're just a brain, right?

THEMES: STEREOTYPES, FRIENDSHIP, FLIRTING

Callback
Bill Svanoe

Play Synopsis: *Callback* is a two character contemporary dramatic comedy, about the forty-year mostly professional relationship between an actress and a director. They both go through struggles, heartbreaks, triumphs, and unexpected discoveries along the way. They are bound together on and off by many things, but what keeps them both going is their overwhelming love of the theater.

Character: Judy
Age: 20s
Genre: Comedic

Scene Synopsis: Judy, nervous and late for an audition, tries to explain why she was delayed, and makes more of an impression than she realizes.

Notes:

Callback

JUDY. Let me explain why I'm late. Last week I got on the Sixth Avenue IRT to go to my acting class. I'm studying with Michael by the way. So I'm sitting on the train reading *An Actor Prepares*, such amazing information. Have you read it? I was in the first car where I always sit, when the whole train came to a screeching halt right in the middle of nowhere. I began to panic. This amazing pressure began to build right here. Then the lights went out. It was so quiet nobody said anything. I wanted to scream but then I didn't want to indicate my location to any possible miscreants on board. Then out of the darkness comes a voice over the intercom; "Don't worry; everything's all right." Everything's all right? We're stuck in a black hole under a billion pounds of rock, leaky pipes, frayed cables, rats the size of rottweilers, alligators… What would be this guy's idea of everything not being all right?

Oh, I'm sorry. I know you're busy. Here's my picture and resume.

> (**JUDY** *pulls her picture out of her purse and manages to dump the entire contents of her purse on the stage. Things clang and roll everywhere.* **JUDY** *stares silently at the carnage for a moment.*)

I'm so embarrassed. I guess I'm more nervous than I realized. I know it's good to be nervous, but uncoordinated…. I guess it's a good thing this part doesn't call for dancing or swordplay.

THEMES: FEAR, NERVES, HOPE

Angry Young Women in Low Rise Jeans with High Class Issues

Matt Morillo

Play Synopsis: This comedy is told in five outrageously funny parts all dealing with young women and the various issues they confront today. Coffee-driven, sensitive, wired, misunderstood, and fuming with awkward issues, these girls are frustrated with the ways of the world, the perceptions men have of them and their own complex reactions to it.

Character: Soleil
Age: 20s – 30s
Genre: Comedic

Scene Synopsis: Soleil gives a very interesting presentation in a conference room in New York City.

Notes:

Angry Young Women in Low Rise Jeans with High Class Issues

SOLEIL. I remember when I was eighteen and shaving wasn't "in" yet. My boyfriend at the time asked me to shave it and I told him no because the idea of sticking a razor down there or waxing it seemed sadistic. But now, not only do I shave it, I periodically pay a complete stranger to tear my pubes out with hot wax and gauze strips while I lay spread eagle on a table with Enya playing in the background. What the fuck? You know when I knew we were nearing the apocalypse? When my mother started shaving her vagina. Oh yeah. I'm not joking. My mother is a fifty-five year old grandmother and she grooms herself into one of those disgusting landing strip things. Oh my God it's so gross. In fact, the other day she offered to treat me to a Brazilian bikini wax. Not only does that mean she was thinking about my vagina, she was thinking about styling it. Nice mother-daughter bonding activity, huh? Fathers and sons go to the ball game together while mothers and daughters get their twats trimmed together. How nice. And here's the kicker on that one. Back in the 60's, my mom was a feminist who burned her bras. I actually remember when I was a little girl and she didn't even shave her armpits. Isn't that something? I mean when did this happen? I thought the whole idea of feminism is to be known for your mind instead of your hoo ha. I'm serious. When did being a strong independent woman cease to be a cool thing to do? And why do we continue to conform? Is it for men? Christ, I hope not because let's be honest, no guy is going to turn down sex just because your jeans come up to your waist or because you have a big old muff or because your underwear covers your whole ass. Am I right?

Election Day
Josh Tobiessen

Play Synopsis: It's election day, and Adam knows his over-zealous girlfriend will never forgive him if he fails to vote. But when his sex starved sister, an eco-terrorist, and a mayoral candidate willing to do anything for a vote all show up, Adam finds that making that quick trip to the polls might be harder than he thought. *Election Day* is a hilarious dark comedy about the price of political (and personal) campaigns.

Character: Brenda
Age: 20s – 30s
Genre: Comedic

Scene Synopsis: A hyper and slightly paranoid Brenda tells Adam, her boyfriend, all about her run-in with the law.

Notes:

Election Day

BRENDA. No, it's ok Adam. I am on drugs.

Ok now, hang on and hear me out. There was this big bag of narcotical materials, that I may have eaten. Unintentionally Well, no, fine, intentionally, but because of the police.

Ok ok ok. Earlier today, I found myself to be in possession of a sandwich bag, containing no sandwich, but rather a certain quantity of a controlled substance. When I was in the car later on, a police officer of the law, attemptedly tried to pull me over, and I reacted in such a way as to not go to jail. So, I ate, and eventually consumed, the inner contents of the aforementioned sandwich bag, therefore inebriating the evidence.

In a sense he didn't pull me over and actually was probably not following me, just driving on the same road. As me. Not impossibly in the opposite direction. But, however, it is important to note that for the previous half hour I have been locationed in Starbucks drinking shots of espresso, so I'm fine.

THEMES: Survival, Secrets, Fear

The Receptionist
Adam Bock

Play Synopsis: At the start of a typical day in the Northeast Office, Beverly deals effortlessly with ringing phones and her colleague's romantic troubles. But the appearance of a charming rep from the Central Office disrupts the friendly routine. And as the true nature of the company's business becomes apparent, *The Receptionist* raises disquieting, provocative questions about the consequences of complicity with evil.

Character: Beverly
Age: 20s – 30s
Genre: Comedic

Scene Synopsis: Cheerful and talkative, Beverly tries to make nice with the handsome, charming representative from the Central Office.

Notes:

The Receptionist

BEVERLY. That is a good pen.

And popular. Make sure you give that back to me. People keep stealing my pens. And my highlighters. I can never hold onto them. Highlighters especially. And those Flexors. They walk out of here. I had to put a lock on the supplies drawer. Lorraine would walk away with a three-hole punch if I didn't have eyes like a hawk.

I used to have three people working under me.

Before I came to this office. I've been here for more than two years. I like the people but the office. This chair is terrible. It's. But I don't dare ask for a new one. I should have asked Steve but they reassigned him before I. And I don't dare ask the new person. Randy I think? Because I don't want to be a person who makes a fuss.

And there should be a window. It looks bare, doesn't it. That's why I bring in the flowers. They cheer the place up.

There's no reason for it to look like a funeral parlor in here. The carpet is terrible. Isn't it? Not my colors really. But. Not much I can do.

And I came in yesterday and there were five jams in the copier. Five! Five! Someone just left it like that. Can you? It was probably Lorraine. The copier can be overwhelming.

I'm supposed to get two breaks a day. But I don't take them. I like to work. I'm a worker. My last office, everyone got let go. Except me. I got reassigned. I have a talent that way. Or a curse. Or a talent.

(Laughs.)

I got moved here. What do you do at the central office?

THEMES: WORK, SURVIVAL, ROUTINE

Baggage
Sam Bobrick

Play Synopsis: Two difficult, single people, Phyllis and Bradley, both trying to heal from their respective disappointing relationships, get their luggage mixed up at the airport. After a very disagreeable first encounter, the two decide to help each other get over their heartaches by forcing a friendship that eventually leads to the two discovering that while they may be too difficult for everyone else in the world, they are right for each other.

Character: Phyllis
Age: 30s
Genre: Comedic

Scene Synopsis: Phyllis, during a session with her therapist, talks about Bradley, a stranger she met due to a luggage mishap and who she immediately disliked. Slightly desperate and near giving up on relationships all together, Phyllis decides the only way to make it work is to force it.

Notes:

THEMES: DATING, LOVE, CONTROL

Baggage

PHYLLIS. Let me explain how I've been thinking. Here I am, a very cautious, unattached, independent, not unattractive, woman, with no guy in sight and not getting any younger. Okay, along comes Bradley Naughton, a guy who is not bad looking, clean, apparently no criminal record, has a good job, is emotionally needy and ripe for the picking with only one slight problem. He's not my type. So here's my plan. It's very simple. I will turn Bradley Naughton into my type. George Bernard Shaw sort of did that in *Pygmalion* and that worked out fine. It's not going to be that difficult. He's already beaten down so the resistance will be almost nil. I will simply win his confidence, make him very dependent on me and what I don't like about him, I'll change. In no time at all, Bradley Naughton will be the perfect man for me. Trust me, when I finish with him you will like him so much more than you do now. And what about his hang up with his ex-wife? Well, did you listen to him? In all the time he kept crying and moaning about missing her, did you once hear the word "love" mentioned? I didn't. That should tell you something. Anyway, I think it's a positive opportunity. Devious? Underhanded? Unethical? Yes. But in today's market, not a bad option for a single girl over thirty. Especially one as spirited and picky and terrified about relationships as myself. Okay, I know what you're thinking. What about love on my part? Well, I've been living without it so far and as you can see, it hasn't affected me in the least. But it's time for me to settle down and I do believe Bradley and I can have a very nice life together. I promise you, it's going to work out fine.

THEMES: DATING, LOVE, CONTROL

Last Chance Romance
Sam Bobrick

Play Synopsis: Myra Witzer, a strong willed woman in her late thirties, is determined to get married at any cost and Leonard Shank, an unassuming man in his early forties is the guy she goes after and gets, much against his will. After several months of married life, Myra realizes that the chase excited her more than the capture and wants out. On the other hand, Leonard, who at the beginning wanted no part of the marriage to Myra, now wants to stay married to her more than anything.

Character: Myra
Age: 30s
Genre: Comedic

Scene Synopsis: After a minor incident that happened while at the theatre together, Myra goes to visit her date, Leonard, in the hospital. Still convinced they are meant to be together, Myra tries to make amends for a small accident she may or may not have caused.

Notes:

THEMES: DATING, LOVE, CONFUSION

Last Chance Romance

MYRA. Please, Leonard. I did not push you off the balcony. It was the end of act one, I needed to go to the bathroom badly and you were blocking the way. I tried to scoot behind you and well, it didn't work out. I tell you, in a New York theater if you don't get to the ladies room fast, you have to wait forever. They really have to do something about that situation. Maybe I'll mention that too in my letter to the *Times*. Anyway, Leonard, you didn't miss anything. The actors were so unnerved by your accident, their timing was off and the second act didn't seem to work as well as the first.

I knew if you lived you'd want to know how the play ended. I mean I wasn't worried that you wouldn't live but with the substandard conditions of the hospitals and the doctors all being unhappy about insurance payments; you never know what could happen. I've been telling people for years, if you don't have to go to the hospital, don't go. Anyway, I'm happy to say you're looking much better than the Edelmans... The couple you fell on. They're just beginning to feel sensations in their feet and the wife is almost able to speak whole sentences.

I beg you, Leonard, don't make me feel any worse than I do. By the way, that wasn't Al Pacino you saw. I checked it out. He was in France at the time attending a film festival. *(Holds out flower pot.)* Oh, this is for you. I didn't think you were into flowers so I got this instead. If you water it every day in two months you'll have all the oregano you'll ever need.

The Idiot Box
Michael Elyanow

Play Synopsis: *The Idiot Box* tells the story of six sitcom characters whose lives are shaken when reality crashes into their perfect world. As the artifice of their lives unravels, each character discovers powerful truths about race, love, sexuality and the America outside they never knew existed.

Character: Stephanie
Age: 30s
Genre: Comedic

Scene Synopsis: On the verge of having a nervous breakdown, Stephanie, a romance novelist, calls up a famous author to try to get some advice about the current book she's working on. However, her writer's block might be caused by more than just the characters in her story.

Notes:

The Idiot Box

STEPHANIE. Hello? HellohMYGODhello! I've been on hold so long I wasn't sure if I got disconnected but I don't think I did if this is you, LaVyrle, IS this you, LaVyrle, do you mind if I call you LaVyrle? Um, oh, it's me, Ms. Spencer: Stephanie Dash. No-no-no-no, don't hang up! I know I shouldn't be calling you at home, but I got your number from – well, I don't want to get anybody fired – just please. I, I don't know how much your cleaning lady told you, but I'm a romance novelist like you – okay, not like you, I don't have 15 million copies in print or a deal with Lifetime – yet, hahaha – BUT. *(Breaks down.)* I'm blocked, Ms. Spencer. I've been in this office for 41 days straight and haven't written a word, stuck in the same scene I've been trying to get through for over a year. It's this scene, this scene where my leading lady, a cool modern businesswoman, right, has been dating this guy, Tom, who she met at this charity event, and everybody loves Tom because he's Tom, quirky loveable helpful Tom, who just asked her to marry him but, the thing is, she won't say yes. I mean, she's supposed to. To say yes. Otherwise I have no story. But. Every time I type it out, Y-E-S, it comes out N-O! N-O! Like my fingers won't let me type it cuz it's not true to the character, y'know? And he's not bad, this guy, Connor, I mean Tom, it's just, I think my lead gets that he's not right for her. Y'know? So she won't let me type Y-E-S, cuz whenever she's around Connor-Tom-Fuck he turns her into this thing that she's not – controlling and mean and naggy – and I'm sure Connor doesn't mean to do it but he does and I don't hate my husband, I don't, but I hate the person that I am with him, y'know, the person that I've become and I swear to you I'm not that person, I'm not an asshole but what am I supposed to do, LaVyrle? Because I'm not giving up on Love. I write about Love. I need Love. And if give that up, if I give up Love… I have no husband, no marriage, no career, and then what? What am I left with? What the fuck do I have then, LaVyrle?

From Up Here
Liz Flahive

Play Synopsis: Kenny Barrett did something that has everyone worried. He wishes he could just make it through the rest of his senior year unnoticed, but that's going to be hard since he has to publicly apologize to his entire high school. At home, his mother is struggling with a rocky start to her second marriage and a surprise visit from her estranged sister. A play about a family limping out the door in the morning and coming home no matter what.

Character: Grace
Age: 40s
Genre: Comedic

Scene Synopsis: Grace can't figure out how to help her son, and when a stranger is able to reach out to her child in a way he won't let her, she has a slight emotional breakdown, which she describes to her husband: in the police station.

Notes:

From Up Here

GRACE. I was sitting in the kitchen alone and I...I couldn't be in that house anymore, I couldn't be in there so I walked outside to get some air and calm down. And those gardeners were finishing replanting next door after that pipe burst and they were packing up. So I walked over to check in with Bonnie, see if everything was alright and I see this man, one of the gardeners on our lawn. He was hiding in the bushes on the side of the house. And his pants were down. And he was going to the bathroom. On my lawn. On our lawn. He's outside, exposed, on my lawn, quietly shitting on my lawn, like it wasn't anything, like this was something he did all the time, like crouching behind a hydrangea bush made him invisible. And I ran over there screaming, I was screaming, and you know I can really scream, you've never actually heard me scream. It's so loud. Shocked the hell out of me. And I ran up to him and I kicked him. Hard. Right in the ankle. All the time screaming and screaming. I guess all the other women in the neighborhood turn a blind eye because his face... He looked so surprised. And I started hitting him with my hands and I grabbed his shirt and pushed him down and put his face right near his mess and I said, you're going to clean that up, you don't shit on people's lawns. Who do you think you are? I live here. My family lives here. And he started crying, saying something I couldn't understand, full of shame and anger. And then I started crying, apologizing to him over and over so now we're both there. Sobbing. And that was when I went back inside and I started throwing everything away. I'd see something and I'd pick it up, take it outside and drop it at the curb. Plates, furniture, pictures, all your clothes. And then I knocked down the mailbox. And that was really satisfying so I knocked down the Kirschenbaum's mailbox across the street. Then...well then the police came over. And brought me here. That's what happened to me. How was your day? What happened to you?

THEMES: FAMILY, FRUSTRATION, CONTROL

Hat Tricks
Dori Appel

Play Synopsis: *Hat Tricks* is an exciting compilation of six scenes and three monologues designed for performance by mature actresses, covering a range of women's experiences in the second half of life. This is a richly varied collection featuring a single intriguing commonality: Every scene or monologue includes the presence and compelling use of a HAT!

Character: Eleanor
Age: 50s – 60s
Genre: Comedic

Scene Synopsis: Eleanor is delivering a speech at the local community center. Her topic: "New Horizons for Older Adults." However, she is having a little trouble following her train of thought and reading her note cards.

Notes:

THEMES: AGING, FAMILY, FRUSTRATION

Hat Tricks

ELEANOR. In case you want to know, I had perfect twenty-twenty vision until I was nearly forty-six! That's when I got my first reading glasses – a blow to my pride, maybe, but not what you'd call a tragedy. After all, everybody wears them, and if you lose them, you just pick up another pair at the drug store! But, of course, it didn't stop there! Around the time I turned fifty I found I couldn't read the telephone directory, even with my glasses on. – So I got stronger glasses, which then made the computer screen all blurry. – Oh, don't get me started on the computer. The only reason I have one at all is so I can email my kids and do a little shopping. Anyway, I started using the first glasses for the computer and the stronger ones for reading, which was only a little confusing – but then a few months ago the trees began to look funny. At first, I thought maybe they all had some kind of pestilence that was causing their leaves to fuse together, because they looked like those drawings kids make – no individual leaves, just cloud-shaped blobs of green. So now I've got to wear distance glasses in addition to my reading glasses and my computer glasses – and I can't handle it! I've got them all on different colored cords – green for distance, purple for the computer and chopping vegetables, red for reading, but I always seem to pick the wrong one. Which is why I finally decided to get trifocals. I just picked them up at the optometrist yesterday, but since I was supposed to give this talk, I thought I'd better stick to what I'm used to – and now look what a mess I've made of everything! Obviously I should have trusted technology more and worn my trifocals in the first place. *(She begins groping in her purse.)* I've got them here somewhere. *(She gropes and frantically pats various pockets and… finally clutches her head.)* I give up! I give up! *(She discovers the trifocals on top of her head.)* Oh, here they are! As I was saying, as we grow older it becomes necessary to find a new vision of the world and our place in it.

DRAMATIC MONOLOGUES

MALE

Sunken Living Room
David Caudle

Play Synopsis: November, 1978. Wade Minnick, 16, is a slender, effeminate bookworm in suburban Miami. With his distracted mother out playing Bridge, and his pilot father away on a trip, his volatile brother Chip, 17, takes off on a dubious errand, leaving Wade alone with Chip's foxy pothead girlfriend. "Freak" Tammy teaches "brain" Wade more about life and about himself than he could learn from a dozen novels.

Character: Chip
Age: Teens
Genre: Dramatic

Scene Synopsis: Chip returns home ready for a fight and set on leaving town. He tears up the house in search of money while his brother tries to stop him. After nearly strangling him, Chip confides in his brother.

Notes:

Sunken Living Room

CHIP. Dad's got some major low-hangin balls, tellin me I should never be a father. Not just right now. Not just with Tammy. Never. Look what a shitty job he's doin! Look at us. Look at us right now. And who knows where the hell Allison is, or what shape she's in. This is a fuckin disaster. And he's gonna tell me...I coulda had that kid. I coulda taken care of 'im, and taught 'im things, and he woulda thought I could do no wrong. And when he got older, I woulda let 'im go out for sports and fuckin lose every single time if he sucked, just so long as he kept tryin. And if he didn't wanna go for sports, I'da made sure he did real good in school, so he could do whatever he wanted to do with his life. Even if he was fat, or ugly. I wouldn'a cared. And when he grew up, I'da wanted him to have kids, so a part of him would keep goin on. He'da been somethin special. He'da made somethin outta himself. He'd a made somethin outta me.

THEMES: Family, Failure, Control

Billboard
Michael Vukadinovich

Play Synopsis: Andy, a recent college graduate weighed down by student loans, gets paid a great deal to tattoo a corporate logo on his forehead. The decision has both tragic and comic consequences as he comes to learn that the logo is more than just ink on his skin. *Billboard* is a comedy about the battle between commercialism, fame, art and love.

Character: Damon
Age: 20s
Genre: Dramatic

Scene Synopsis: In light of the trouble Andy and his girlfriend Katelyn are having over Andy's new tattoo, Damon reflects in a direct address to the audience about the first time he met Katelyn, how something small can change your life, and how art – in all forms – can deeply affect people.

Notes:

Billboard

DAMON. The first time I met Katelyn was at my Dad's funeral
five years ago. Andy waited weeks before he introduced me
to her. That's how I knew it was serious. The girls he didn't
care about he'd let me meet right away. It was an unusual
first meeting of course, but the thing was that while I was
feeling awful about my dad, she was the only one who
said anything to me that made me feel any better. Here,
my friend's new girlfriend, made me feel better than any
of my family or friends with just a few words. Sometimes a
stranger can do so much more for us than those close to
us. After my Dad's death I was especially worried about my
Mom because she didn't cry. It wasn't a sudden death, my
Father was sick for some time, but I still thought she should
be crying. Later, after I moved back home, Katelyn gave me
a small painting. There was no real image in the painting.
Just shape and color. I liked it so I hung it in our living
room. When my mom walked in she looked at it and immediately burst into tears. I don't know what she saw in it but
the affect was immediate and in a way I don't understand
it helped her. Without Andy and Katelyn I don't think I
would have dealt with any of it very well. Sometimes when
I imagine my own funeral – I'll probably die of cancer
because everyone dies of cancer – I think how cool it would
be if everyone brought paint and wrote messages and drew
pictures all over my casket like kids do on their friend's
casts after they break a bone. They could write stories or
draw memories and it might help people cry. How absurd
that we need help crying! But the tears would mix with the
paint and the result might be amazing.

Lizards
Megan Mostyn-Brown

Play Synopsis: A near-drowning accident sends Phoebe into a tailspin as she turns away from her marriage and toward her rescuer. Science teacher Victor loses his job and meets an unusual girl all in one day. While Ronnie is deciding whether to tell her newly single roommate Sebastian how she really feels. Through a masterful web of intertwined storylines and relationships, *Lizards* tells the tale of six twenty-somethings adapting to stress – and on the brink of change.

Character: Jesse
Age: 20s
Genre: Dramatic

Scene Synopsis: Jesse and his wife are struggling with her near-drowning, and are drifting further away from each other. Jesse confides in a co-worker his greatest fear – that she still hasn't resurfaced, and maybe never will.

Notes:

Lizards

JESSE. She's disappeared…not literally… I mean she's still at home… a human being sitting there… but she's gone… the Phoebe I knew is gone… inside I guess… I mean I look at her…. into her fuckin' eyes and there's nothing there… I mean there's something there but nothing I recognize… and I keep thinking about our honeymoon… not in some sad, romantic things were blissful kind of way… but in this – see, we went to Scotland and took this boat tour of Loch Ness… ya know that place where the monster supposedly is… and anyway she wandered to the other end of the boat and this guy started telling me… just me mind you… that the monster isn't a monster it's actually these reptiles that live at the bottom of the lake… and the lake is really dense… so dense that you can't see the bottom… and that these reptiles that live in the lake they swim around all happy and shit but when they lose their way that's when they come to the surface… to orient themselves… that's when we see them ya know… when they're lost… anyway I guess I just keep hoping that happens with Phoebe, cuz she's lost… and I can't seem to find her in there… in all that denseness beneath her eyes… and I hope whatever it is comes to the surface… I just want her to come to the surface….

New York
David Rimmer

Play Synopsis: David Rimmer, a Pulitzer Prize finalist author for *Album*, originally wrote *New York* to raise funds for volunteer psychiatrists dedicated to helping the overwhelming number of patients psychologically affected by 9/11. Depicting the reactions of 15 individuals to the events of that day, the characters all speak to a central psychiatrist.

Character: Fireman
Age: 20s – 30s
Genre: Dramatic

Scene Synopsis: A fireman dealing with the aftermath of 9/11 confesses to his psychiatrist how confused his life has become. Others have started relying on him to cope with the tragedy, but does he have the strength to support them as well as deal with his own trauma?

Notes:

New York

FIREMAN. Everything's crazy – People come up to me like I'm a god or something. This one lady, she saw me on the street. She just touched me. Right here.

(Holds out his arm.)

That's all she wanted to do. Like I could heal her or something She didn't even look sick. I've been interviewed by every single news agency known to man. Derek Jeter's my new best friend, Alec Baldwin calls me twice a day, I have heart-to-heart talks with Susan Sarandon.

"Tommy, what should I do? Should I take the second biggest part in the new Woody Allen movie?"

"Susan, I love the Woodman, but babe… c'mon…"

What do these people want – ?

Yesterday, I'm workin' on The Pile, y'know – I look up…

(Sings.)

"Here she comes… Miss America…" I'm not kiddin' – the crown, the sash, the whole thing – just in case we didn't know.

I got so many girlfriends now I can't keep 'em straight. One of 'em actually likes me. We were walking in her neighborhood the other day and we go past Barney's. What's in the window? A fireman mannequin – in the uniform – ax, helmet. Right next to him, a Fire Department sweatshirt, for sale. Fireman Chic – T-shirts everywhere. DKNY – FDNY – what's the difference? – Why was it them and not me? Why am I here? And they're – Pure stupid luck. They kept going back in. Right into the smoke.

Circuitry
Andrew Barrett

Play Synopsis: *Circuitry* is an outrageously funny, unapologetic ninety-minute play that takes us on a yearlong whirlwind global trip through the exclusive world of the Circuit Party. It is part realism and part absurdism and totally fabulous as it follows one gay New Yorker's quest for love through this seductive world in 1996. As HIV/AIDS remains a major part of the gay community worldwide, *Circuitry* takes a glimpse backwards to question the state of a large group of gay men today.

Character: Brian
Age: 20s – 30s
Genre: Dramatic

Scene Synopsis: Brian's partner, Paul, is dying. With the prospect of going to the hospital again, and maybe not coming back, Paul asks Brian what he will do while he's gone this time.

Notes:

Circuitry

BRIAN. It's seven p.m. The last customer has left the store. I turn the 'closed' sign around. I lower the lights, just enough to make it feel like candle glow. I turn on the CD Player and listen to Sade. I take a deep breath and I smell the hundreds of years collected in all of the dust. I walk very slowly, aisle by aisle, and I run my finger along the spine of each book. I feel its individuality. Its imperfections. I feel its value to someone else. I feel the power it holds that draws an unsuspecting lover. One night, Saturday night, while you're in the hospital, one book, will grab my attention. It will lure my hand to pull it out. To take it and feel more than the surface. It will be a first edition *Wuthering Heights*. Priceless. In my hands. I'll put it to my ear like a seashell to hear all those who have cried for Cathy and Heathcliff. I will feel the salty, wetness drip down my neck. The back of my hand will catch a drop and I'll taste it. I'll fall to my knees and give myself entirely to the gift. Alone in the store, in the candle lit darkness with the sounds of Sade I'll lay on the floor and hold the ancient text open to reveal its innermost secrets. I'll lay there for as long as it will seduce me. It will last all night. Then I'll rise up. My head will spin in euphoria. I'll have smelt the lovelorn air. I'll have tasted the passionate tears. I'll have heard the yearning voice. And I'll only be thinking of you.

Additional Particulars
Ed Simpson

Play Synopsis: The intersecting lives of four "Save-a-Bundle Discount Mart" employees are explored in *Additional Particulars*. In the first act, Glenda Balitski, an optimistic but lonely young woman has recently moved into her tidy apartment after the death of her invalid mother. Assistant Manager Warren Grippo, a generous but awkward man of unflagging good manners, has unexpectedly dropped by Glenda's apartment after work.

Character: Warren
Age: 30s
Genre: Dramatic

Scene Synopsis: Warren enthusiastically shares his feelings about the company for which he works while revealing a little about himself to the woman of his dreams.

Notes:

Additional Particulars

WARREN. I don't think you could find a better place to work. You see, I have an associate degree in business –

(With great pride.) Allegheny County Community College. Yes, indeed. Anyway, when I received my degree, I interviewed with a number of companies and, let me tell you, Glenda, some pretty heavy hitters, too. Established national chains. But I was looking for a dynamic, growing company where I could step right in and make a difference. With SaveaBundle, I found – if you will – a professional home. I could tell from the first interview. You know, most people are interested in how a company can help them. Not me. I talked to Ted Crandall from the main office and I just asked, point blank "How can I help? What can I do to contribute?" Well, let me tell you, that surprised him. That, I think, he found refreshing, you know? He hesitated for a moment and you could see he was considering this proposition from all the angles. He had that look, you know? That look he gets when he's carefully looking at all the aspects. You know the look I'm talking about. Well he has this look.

Finally, he looked me right in the eyes, stuck out his hand, and said, "Well, to start out with, you can become a member of our team –" that's what he called it, Glenda, a team – "you can become a member of our team and within three years, you could advance right up the ladder to assistant manager." You know what I said? … "Where do I sign?"

4 years, 2 employee of the month awards, 3 management trainee retreats later – here I am.

THEMES: WORK, PRIDE, STRENGTH

Treasure Island
Ken Ludwig

Play Synopsis: Based on the masterful adventure novel by Robert Louis Stevenson, *Treasure Island* is a stunning yarn of piracy on the tropical seas. At the center of it all are Jim Hawkins, a 14-year-old boy who longs for adventure, and the infamous Long John Silver, perhaps the most famous hero-villain of all time. Silver is an unscrupulous buccaneer-rogue whose greedy quest for gold, coupled with his affection for Jim, cannot help but win the heart of every soul who has ever longed for romance, treasure and adventure.

Character: Rathbone
Age: 30s
Genre: Dramatic

Scene Synopsis: Accused of stealing a much-desired map from Captain Flint, Jemmy Rathbone, caught by his pirate cohorts, gives one last testimony to his innocence – but will it be enough to save his life?

Notes:

Treasure Island

RATHBONE. Billy Bones, sir,

No he ain't dead. Ya thought he was dead, we all did.

But that night after the treasure was buried

And the men what buried it put to death,

Well I was watch that night and around about

Three bells I hears a noise, and afore I knows it

There comes Billy Bones a-clamberin' over

The side o' the ship – 'e 'ad survived, ya see –

And he limps to your quarters and he steals the map!

And then I – I stops him like, right here on this deck,

And I says "Give me the map! That there belongs to

Captain Flint, the very man what gave me

Me start in this most noble o' professions."

'Cause it's like I worships you, Cap'n. You're my

Hero like.

    (In tears.)

He threatens me, and says that if I ever

Says a word about it, then he'll track

Me down and kill me. And then he was over the side

Like that!

THEMES: SURVIVAL, GREED, ALLEGIANCE

Nest
Bathsheba Doran

Play Synopsis: Based on historical fact, *Nest* is a taut domestic love triangle set against the landscape of a fledgling nation on the verge of realizing its manifest destiny at a terrible bloody cost. The play re-imagines the real life story of Susanna Cox, a young indentured servant from Pennsylvania who murdered her baby in 1809, and the story of the man who wrote the ballad that was sold at her hanging. The play is a searing exploration of American dreams and violence and their place in the national psyche.

Character: Chaplain
Age: 30s
Genre: Dramatic

Scene Synopsis: The Chaplain tries to reach out to Jacob, who has strayed from more than just the Church. Knowing that Jacob prefers the logic of philosophers to religion, the Chaplain still tries to make a case for Faith.

Notes:

THEMES: FAITH, RELIGION, TEMPTATION

Nest

CHAPLAIN. Jacob, it is by prayer and prayer alone that you will come to know God. Not by reading French radicals. Those of us in the business recommend that you come to church every week, and pray with us, in a group, even if you don't believe. It is through that process, you will find Him. Because, and I have to tell you this as a member of my flock, we believe that not doing so can be quite costly. In terms of the hereafter. *(A beat.)*

You know, there is a minister in New York who is said to perform miracles. He held his hands above a woman whose flesh was covered in sores. He remained that way for over an hour and her wounds began to dry up.

Sometimes I catch myself thinking that the whole of the Bible took place on a great big cloud and was never anything more than make believe made by God to make us believe. But then I remember it all happened right here on earth. Jesus was a man. Just like us. He struggled as we do, and raged as we do. They all did. Abraham. His father Terrah, who came home one day to a house full of broken idols and a son who claimed to have met the one true God. They were all just men. Like us. Struggling to know God. Here on earth. Which is why on this very globe you may find Golgotha, or Eden, or the skeleton of Noah's ark. Because it all happened right here. And it is still happening.

I can feel God. I can feel him pulling me towards him. Is the path stony? Yes. Are my feet bleeding? Yes. Am I starving and naked, is it dark and cold? You bet. But I know that's God up ahead, shining like a sunrise. And when I die, I'll be met on the other side by someone who loves me. And everything will clarify.

Outrage
Itamar Moses

Play Synopsis: In Ancient Greece, Socrates is accused of corrupting the young with his practice of questioning commonly held beliefs. In Renaissance Italy, a simple miller named Menocchio runs afoul of the Inquisition when he develops his own theory of the cosmos. In Nazi Germany, the playwright Bertolt Brecht is persecuted for work that challenges authority. And in present day New England, a graduate student finds himself in the center of a power struggle over the future of the University. An irreverent epic that spans thousands of years, *Outrage* explores the power of martyrdom, the power of theatre, and how the revolutionary of one era becomes the tyrant of the next.

Character: Daniel Rivnine
Age: 30s
Genre: Dramatic

Scene Synopsis: Daniel Rivnine, an English professor, practices a lecture he plans on giving to his class.

Notes:

Outrage

DANIEL RIVNINE. Why does Eve eat the apple?

It's a good question. Her whole world is God, who has told her to obey Adam, and Adam, who has told her to obey God. And yet Satan, in the guise of a talking snake, changes her mind. He says:

Why then was this forbid? Why but to awe

Why but to keep ye low and ignorant

His worshippers; he knows that in the day

Ye eat thereof, your Eyes that seem so cleere

Yet are but dim, shall perfetly be then

Op'nd and cleerd, and ye shall be as Gods...

Satan is a little biased, of course. Here is a former angel, indeed God's most trusted adviser, cast down for the unforgivable crime of revolutionary activity. He'd grown tired of God's arbitrary rules: All Praise Me; Everyone Play Golden Harps And Sing Major Thirds; and, the last straw, Everyone Worship My Son. And when Satan lost the war in heaven, he looked out over the abyss, God's ferocious forces at his heels, and chose to fling himself over the edge.

Who is the hero of Milton's rendition of Western Civilization's first story? The distant, impulsive, and arrogant God? Dim-witted Adam? Manipulative Eve? God's obedient Son? Every creature here is intellectually blind. Except for one. And he wins. Simply by persuading Adam and Eve to disobey God's edicts *at all,* for spurring them to *act.*

And so: Adam and Eve are cast out. But I say to Hell with it: we're better off. The first moment in this story when anyone does anything remotely Human is when Milton tells us: *Reaching to the Fruit, She pluk'd, She et.* So why does Eve eat the apple? Because the hero teaches her she can. Because he makes her human.

THEMES: Religion, Revolution, Temptation

Jerome Bixby's The Man From Earth
Richard Schenkman

Play Synopsis: History professor John Oldman unexpectedly resigns from the University, and his startled colleagues invite themselves to his home for an explanation. But they're shocked to hear his reason: John claims he must move on because he is immortal, and cannot stay in one place for more than ten years without his secret being discovered. John's fellow professors attempt to poke holes in his story, but it soon becomes clear that his tale is as impossible to disprove as it is to verify.

Character: John
Age: 30s – 40s
Genre: Dramatic

Scene Synopsis: John patiently explains to his friends and colleagues the true reasons behind his decision to retire, and greater truths about his mysterious past.

Notes:

Jerome Bixby's The Man From Earth

JOHN. The Old Testament sells fear and guilt. The New Testament is a great work of ethics, put into my mouth by better philosophers and poets than I am. But the message isn't practiced. The fairy tales build churches.

I called myself John, I almost always do. As tales of the resurrection spread, the name was confused with the Hebrew Yohanan, meaning "God is gracious." My stay on earth was seen as divine proof of immortality. That led to "God is salvation," or in Hebrew, "Yeshua," which in translations became my proper name, changing to the Late Greek Iesous, then to Late Latin Iesus, finally to Medieval Latin Jesus. It was a wonder to watch.

It began as a schoolhouse and ended as a temple. I said I had a Master, who was greater than myself. I wanted to teach what I had learned. I never said he was my father. I never claimed to be king of the Jews, I didn't walk on water, I didn't raise the dead, I never spoke of the divine except in the sense of human goodness on Earth. No wise men came from the East to worship at a manger. I did do a little healing, employing Eastern medicine I'd learned.

I did try some teaching one day, from a hill. Not many stayed to listen.

The biblical Jesus said, "Who do you think I am?" He gave them a choice. I'm giving you one.

Three Musketeers
Ken Ludwig

Play Synopsis: Based on the timeless swashbuckler by Alexandre Dumas, a tale of heroism, treachery, close escapes and above all, honor. The story begins with d'Artagnan who sets off for Paris with Sabine, his sister, who poses as a young man and quickly becomes entangled in her brother's adventures. After reaching Paris, d'Artagnan joins forces with his heroes, the infamous Musketeers Athos, Porthos and Aramis, and finds himself in opposition to Cardinal Richelieu and the deadly Countess de Winter, known as Milady.

Character: Athos
Age: 30s – 40s
Genre: Dramatic

Scene Synopsis: Athos, in telling d'Artagnan a story about a supposed "friend," opens up about a dark past he will not allow himself to look back on, and unwittingly sheds light on revelations to come.

Notes:

Three Musketeers

ATHOS. Falling in love is a fool's game. It leads to nothing but regret. And darkness. And the death of hope – a friend of mine. He was a count then, of the province of Quercy.

He fell in love at the age of twenty-five with a young girl of sixteen, as beautiful as the dawn. She was happy to be alive. She lived in a village with her brother, the local curate. They'd settled there the year before and no one asked from whence they'd come. No one bothered, for she was all good and he was of God. My friend, the count, he could have seduced the girl or even ravished her at his will. But no, he was a man of 'honour' – and so he married her. Then he took her to his home and worshipped her and gave her jewels and carriages and they were happy. So very happy. Then one day they were out hunting together and she took a fall. The horse threw her recklessly and she lost consciousness. The man rushed to help her, and seeing that her riding habit was tight and stifling, he slit it open with a knife. And there, on her shoulder, was a fleur-delis. She was branded.

She was a thief. A convict. And so this man, this sovereign ruler of his province with rights of criminal and of civil justice, he tied her hands behind her back, and with a good stout rope, he hanged her from a tree.

He changed his name and was never heard from again. But it is said that he has spent his life fighting evil to purge his sin. And now it's time to get drunk. *(To the tavern keeper.)* More wine! Hey! A stoup of wine!

Dead City
Sheila Callaghan

Play Synopsis: Samantha Blossom wakes up one June morning in her Upper East Side apartment to find her life being narrated over the airwaves of public radio. She discovers in the mail an envelope addressed to her husband from his lover, which spins her raw and untethered into an odyssey through the city. This 90 minute comic drama is a modernized, gender-reversed, relocated, hyper-theatrical riff on the novel *Ulysses*.

Character: Gabriel
Age: 40s
Genre: Dramatic

Scene Synopsis: Gabriel – feeling confused and alone, tries to find a way to re-connect with his wife. He wants to understand her, or at least try to, but the distance between them has grown. Only now, when she is fast asleep in bed, is he able to confront her – without her hearing one word of what he says.

Notes:

Dead City

GABRIEL. I saw you the other day when you were in your office, I came home early from the gym and you had that little box on your screen, the one that makes noises and you think I don't know what it is but it's something you use to talk to other people, and you hit a key and a picture of a rain forest popped up on your screen and for some reason you thought I wouldn't realize the forest was there to cover whatever it was you were talking about, and I want to tell you that I am COMPLETELY fine with it, I mean lord knows you can do whatever you want, but I want to talk about it, you know, I mean I don't want to know details or anything but it might be nice just to kind of get a sense I mean is he YOUNG or OLD I don't even know are there SEVERAL or just one and where do you two go because I don't think you've ever brought him here and hotels are so expensive I just don't see you wasting a load of cash on someone you barely know but maybe you maybe you're in love. I always thought I'd be able to sense that sort of thing. Is he smarter than me? What do you talk about? Art and politics and all that crap you always try to get me to talk about? Does he have more money than me? I mean I don't really care but see these are the things I wonder when you put up a rain forest to cover yourself.

Everythings Turning into Beautiul
Seth Zvi Rosenfeld

Play Synopsis: This play with music takes place late one Christmas Eve in lonely New York City, when a couple of down-on-their-luck songwriting partners, hitless, loveless and facing their forties, come together for a night of composing and soul searching. Sam and Brenda don't want to compromise their friendship or their working relationship, but this evening will put their partnership to the test.

Character: Sam
Age: 40s
Genre: Dramatic

Scene Synopsis: Brenda and Sam talk about their careers, their failed relationships and what is happening between them. Brenda asks Sam to share a secret with her, and afraid of ruining what they have between them, Sam tries to open up.

Notes:

Everythings Turning into Beautiul

SAM. Okay…When I was a kid in this game and ya know I was supposed to be the next big somebody, right. It was cool. I partied with all my heroes. Got gifts from people I didn't know. Man, they threw parties for me. I remember one time in LA A&M threw a party for me at the Roxbury. Prince was there, Eddie Murphy, Wilt Chamberlain…I'm in the VIP and it's all these people and I don't know any of them, really. I found myself thinking about who my people are. Are my family my people? My mom, is she my people? My girl? I'm high and shit and I'm thinkin' who are my people…Who are my people?…These people look good They keep telling me how talented I am. They must be my people…Am I my people?…Am I my people?…Cause I got this hole inside of me that I wake up with every morning and if these people find out…How broken I really am… And that was the moment…I knew that I'd find a way to fuck this whole thing up.

The secret part is that I just never felt like much…Ya know?….So like you ask me about my marriages and my career and the opportunities I've wasted and ummm…. You know…fuck, God gives everyone a chance to be productive, he opens the fuckin doors you gotta step in and do your job and you don't get a hundred chances…Lots of times you get one great chance. One great chance. One big door opens and you either step all the way the fuck in or you lose…That door opened for me…Widely…and I wasn't wise. I wasn't productive or graceful and so it shut in front of me. That's how I look at it. So if by God's grace that it opens again Brenda. I will be the most productive. I will fulfill my God given potential. Believe that.

Truth and Reconciliation
Etan Frankel

Play Synopsis: It is three years since Lynne and Benjamin Montgomery's son, Ben, traveled to the Central American country of Cartuga. Soon after his arrival, Ben disappeared. In a country of civil strife, guerillas and mass executions by the army, that can mean only one thing – he was killed. So when Bishop Melinda calls to invite the Montgomerys to take part in the historic Cartuga Truth and Reconciliation Commission, they fly down to Central America to find out what happened to their son.

Character: Benjamin Sr.
Age: 50s
Genre: Dramatic

Scene Synopsis: The man responsible for his son's murder is being interviewed by a commission who will, in all probability, grant him amnesty for his statements regarding what happened. Outraged, Benjamin speaks up.

Notes:

Truth and Reconciliation

BENJAMIN SR. I'm not finished, Bishop. I waited my turn. I'm the only one here who apparently finds fault with your little commission. So naive. "Build the future based on a shared memory." *Memory* isn't bringing my son back. And memory sure isn't going to punish this man who killed him. Where I'm from we don't *announce* a man's guilt and then let him *free*. What that is is called *injustice*. Plain and simple. It is taking a wrong and condoning it. And it is unconscionable for you, Bishop, to sit perched on your throne and allow this to happen.

You think that anytime there is conflict and abuse like apartheid in South Africa or oppression here or maybe slavery in my country that you can just cart out your traveling Truth and Reconciliation Commission, roll out the country's Bishop Tutu and publish a report and that solves the problem. That solves nothing. You can't compromise justice with truth. As if we could possibly know the truth anyway. You speak of it as if it's something that can be calculated, like how many oranges you have in a basket. X equals the truth. As if we could ever *really* know.

(Beat.) You speak about creating an environment for reconciliation. What you are doing is solidifying an environment for impunity.

You want to move forward, here's how you do it: show the citizens of this country that a wrong is a wrong and wrongs get punished. That this country is not tolerating abuses anymore. That those that abuse – get punished. It's called a system of justice. And I'll tell you something – no one here's going to believe this place has changed until you show them that the days of injustice *are over*.

This commission cannot force reconciliation! Because reconciliation follows forgiveness. And ONLY I CAN FORGIVE. Me. Alone. And I DO NOT forgive.

The Receptionist
Adam Bock

Play Synopsis: At the start of a typical day in the Northeast Office, Beverly deals effortlessly with ringing phones and her colleague's romantic troubles. But the appearance of a charming rep from the Central Office disrupts the friendly routine. And as the true nature of the company's business becomes apparent, *The Receptionist* raises disquieting, provocative questions about the consequences of complicity with evil.

Character: Mr. Raymond
Age: 50s
Genre: Dramatic

Scene Synopsis: Mr. Raymond, talking to an unseen person, describes a little about himself, and in doing so, paints a much more descriptive picture than, perhaps, he realizes.

Notes:

THEMES: DEATH, FAMILY, WORK

The Receptionist

MR. RAYMOND. My cousin used to take me rabbit hunting. I didn't like it. We'd be out in the woods and I'd spot one. I wouldn't want him to notice it. He used a bow and arrow. They scream. I didn't like it. Me I like fishing. I like fly fishing. There's nothing like it. I love it. I love everything about it. I love watching the line as I cast

You actually throw it back and forth and that curl of line flying out over the water it's

I'd have to show you I wish I could show you You'd love it.

I love reading the stream. Figuring out where the big boys are hanging out. And matching the hatch. And then floating my fly right to them and waiting for them to pop and grab it.

I love catching fish.

I love letting them go too.

I have a philosophy when it comes to a caught fish. If you catch a fish and it's ok, you let it go. But if it's snagged or it's got a hook in its gills you can't put it back in the stream because it'll die. So if that happens I think you should prepare the fish to be killed.

What I do

I bleed the fish It seems a bit gruesome but I cut the gills and I hold it in the water of the stream and bleed it out. It's the humane way to kill a fish. It depletes its oxygen levels and it goes to sleep. And then I eat it. And that's ok. Because everything out there is eating something.

But if I can I let them go.

My wife doesn't fish. She spends her time thinking about the Which I understand. She sees pictures of the people over there and what we're doing to them and she cries. I keep telling her "Don't look at those pictures."

We have friends whose kids are over there. We gotta believe we're doing the right thing. But she

I don't like thinking about it. It makes me sad. It's like we're all trapped in a

When things are hard I think about fly fishing.

THEMES: DEATH, FAMILY, WORK

Trying
Joanna McClelland Glass

Play Synopsis: *Trying* is a two-character play based on the author's experience during 1967-1968 when she worked for Francis Biddle at his home in Washington, D.C. Judge Biddle had been Attorney General of the United States under Franklin Roosevelt. After the war, President Truman named him Chief Judge of the American Military Tribunal at Nuremberg. The play is about a young Canadian girl and an old, Philadelphia aristocrat, "trying" to understand each other in what Biddle knows is the final year of his life.

Character: Judge Biddle
Age: 60s – 70s
Genre: Dramatic

Scene Synopsis: Judge Biddle's new secretary has arrived, and on her first day, he wastes no time in explaining the rules of his office, and setting the tone.

    Notes:

Trying

JUDGE BIDDLE. The tray and the mail have to be lugged by the secretary. It's difficult for me to climb stairs and carry things. I've got a metal pin in my ankle. Did you bring the mail?

It's idiotic, at my age, keeping my office over the garage. Especially since I have to limp across the yard to get here. But houses tend to be seats of domesticity. I learned, very early on, that cerebral efforts haven't a hope in hell in the midst of the women and the ladies. Although I guess that distinction – the women and the ladies – is outmoded now. Obviously, you're cold.

You're cold because you came early, and not when you were told to come. You probably wanted to make a good impression on your first day. You'll find, if you stay, that I'm far more impressed by adherence to rules.

The place is heated by these hideous gas heaters. The operation of them – this is very important – the operation of them must be left entirely to me. We will work mornings only, nine until noon. If I arrive at eight-thirty, and you arrive at nine, I'll have the heaters up and running. *(He sighs, wishing that he was not "obliged" to say the following.)* And I suppose I must add, since employers are obliged to set terms, that if you arrive at nine-fifteen you'll be tardy and I'll be irritable. Now. *(He must bend down to the dial near the floor. As he bends, he leans on the nearby chair. There is pain in the bend and pain in his hand as he turns the dial.)* These damned heaters are as ancient as I am. The imbecile who designed them put the dials down at the floor. I should get something with a wall dial, but I won't go to the expense because I don't expect to last much longer. In fact, I'm fairly certain this is my final year. *(He cannot rise without clutching the chair. He then eyes the far heater, stage left. He starts his shuffle.)* That's the bathroom, over there. If you're like all the others, you'll go in there to cry.

DRAMATIC MONOLOGUES

FEMALE

Billboard
Michael Vukadinovich

Play Synopsis: Andy, a recent college graduate weighed down by student loans, gets paid a great deal to tattoo a corporate logo on his forehead. The decision has both tragic and comic consequences as he comes to learn that the logo is more than just ink on his skin. *Billboard* is a dramatic comedy about the battle between commercialism, fame, art and love.

Character: Katelyn
Age: 20s
Genre: Dramatic

Scene Synopsis: In a direct address to the audience, Katelyn reflects on the reasons a person turns to art, expressing her own struggle with her boyfriend's decision through her story.

Notes:

Billboard

KATELYN. On the plane I sat next to this little girl and her mother. The little girl was drawing with crayons for most of the trip. Pictures of her house and family and pets. Drawings from a child's mind. Every once in a while she would start drawing on the plane, either on the window or the tray, wherever. And her mom would say to her, "Stop drawing on the plane honey. If you can't stay between the lines at least stay on the paper." After awhile I noticed that every time the plane dipped or there was a bit of turbulence she would begin to draw on it. I think it was because she wanted to control the plane. That she thought if she could somehow make it part of her drawing, part of the world she knew, then she would be safe.

When you draw something you seem to somehow understand it better. When I was a little girl, about six or seven – the same as the girl on the plane – I was having bad dreams every night. My parents, both struggling artists, finally decided to pay and send me to a psychiatrist because they were so tired from me sleeping in their bed. The first thing the psychiatrist had me do was draw my nightmares out on paper with crayons. Simply draw my dreams. All the frightening images I had seen the night before in the darkness of sleep. Telling someone your dreams is one thing, but to draw them another. The difference between Freud and Picasso. Those monsters and creatures that made me so scared in bed the night before looked so cartoonish and ridiculous when I drew them out and explained them to her. They were exposed. Out of their darkness. In the light. After only about three or four visits my nightmares stopped completely. They moved from my head to the paper and they were filed away in a cabinet forever.

A Feminine Ending
Sarah Treem

Play Synopsis: *A Feminine Ending* is a gentle, bittersweet comedy about a girl who knows what she wants but not quite how to get it. Her parents are getting divorced, her fiancée is almost famous, her first love reappears, and there's a lot of noise in her head but none of it is music. Until the end.

Character: Amanda
Age: 20s
Genre: Dramatic

Scene Synopsis: When Amanda's mother asks her to come home for the weekend, she agrees. Little does she know that the reason the invitation has come is because her mother wants to tell her that she wants a divorce from Amanda's father. Before finding out, and almost anticipating the discord, Amanda reflects on her family life and the reasons she first wanted to compose music.

Notes:

A Feminine Ending

AMANDA. When I was a girl, around twelve or so – I wanted to write an opera. I knew that Mozart had done it even earlier and hc was a boy, so I figured it couldn't be that hard.

Operas are about love, but at twelve the only person I truly loved was my mother. I thought she was terrific. So I decided to write an opera about her.

When I was young I heard harmony everywhere. The garbage truck harmonized with the lawn mower. The dishwasher harmonized with the air conditioner. My mother harmonized with my father. Their harmony was the most beautiful. Intricate but effortless. Even when they argued. It's all about balance. One voice, one strand, complements the other through contradiction.

Sorry, where were we? Right, my first opera. The one inspired by my mother.

When I sat down to write the glory of my mother, I could not seem to keep her voice far enough away from mine. The notes came out too close to harmonize, though not close enough to synchronize. If my voice came in on A, I would hear her voice, right above me, on A sharp, riding my thread. Every time my voice chose a new direction, her voice would follow the same course but a half-step above or below – as if she was correcting me. Harmonize, I commanded myself. Make them harmonize. But no matter what I did, I could not get the two voices to *listen to each other.*

I gave up on opera after that.

girl.
Megan Mostyn-Brown

Play Synopsis: A play about what it means to be a "girl" in this day and age. The girls in this play show great strength, revealing their vulnerabilities in language that is honest and extremely compelling. Split into three sections, the characters speak entirely in monologues (with some overlap), providing great material for auditions and monologue work.

Character: Lydia
Age: 20s
Genre: Dramatic

Scene Synopsis: Lydia makes some startling confessions, both about the mistakes she has made in her life and – more importantly – the decisions she has made.

Notes:

girl.

LYDIA. Look I'll tell you a
 secret
This was probably the biggest
decision I ever had to make
 You know either way my
  life was gonna be flipped
  sideways
 and
 and
 it took less time
 than
 picking out an outfit for a
  party.
 For real.
 Uhh
 I decided to keep her.
Just like that.
Took about an hour.
Sat in the sink pressing my
 face to the mirror and-
Look you can say what you
 want
because I know there are
 people out there who
would like to
make me the poster child
for some fuckin'
Pro-Life
bullshit
but it wasn't about that
at all.
My shit
much deeper than that.
See
I had no fuckin' plan for my
 life
or even for after graduation
and all the crazy crap going

on made that worse.
I mean everything was so
 fuckin'
ridiculous
and sad
and distant
and empty
and the thought of
having her
was the
one
thing
that seemed right.
Fucked up, huh?
As far as I was concerned
 things couldn't
get any worse.
I couldn't handle them
 getting any worse.
So she had to be a sign of
 something good.
Maybe this was what I was
 supposed to be.
Cuz
sitting there in the sink
with nothing but my breath
and the possibility of her
and what that could be
I dunno
the space between
here *(points to breast)*
and here *(points to thighs)*
finally felt
full
again.
So I kept her.
No political bullshit involved.

THEMES: Sex, Fulfillment, Strength

The Drunken City
Adam Bock

Play Synopsis: Off on the bar crawl to end all crawls, three twenty-something brides-to-be find their lives going topsy-turvy when one of them begins to question her future after a chance encounter with a recently jilted handsome stranger. *The Drunken City* is a wildly theatrical take on the mystique of marriage and the ever-shifting nature of love and identity in a city that never sleeps.

Character: Melissa
Age: 20s
Genre: Dramatic

Scene Synopsis: Tipsy, Melissa talks to the audience about the fragility of emotions; her opinion is due in part to her recent engagement – and her recent heartbreak.

Notes:

The Drunken City

MELISSA. I had everything. I had a ring. It was such a beautiful night the night Jason gave it to me. My hair was up like And Jason looked so shiny and redfaced and he was smiling at me like I was the only person anywhere anywhere anywhere. It was gonna be awesome. And. And we were going to buy a house. I'd already picked it out. It had a gazebo in the backyard. With screens. Where you could put a table in the summer.

Then slowly Like a murmur that I didn't notice at first I couldn't hear it properly I kept hearing these two names. These two names over and over in different low voices. Jason and Jessica. Jessica and Jason.

What kind of name is Jessica anyways Who'd name their kid that? Jessica It's a stupid name.

It was humiliating. I gave my ring back to Jason. And suddenly all over again I had nothing all over again.

THEMES: LOVE, HEARTBREAK, LOSS

Eurydice
Sarah Ruhl

Play Synopsis: In *Eurydice*, Sarah Ruhl reimagines the classic myth of Orpheus through the eyes of its heroine. Dying too young on her wedding day, Eurydice must journey to the underworld, where she reunites with her father and struggles to remember her lost love. With contemporary characters, ingenious plot twists, and breathtaking visual effects, the play is a fresh look at a timeless love story.

Character: Eurydice
Age: 20s
Genre: Dramatic

Scene Synopsis: Eurydice's Father has helped her remember what it was to be alive. Together in the underworld, she talks of her love.

Notes:

Eurydice

EURYDICE. Orpheus never liked words. He had his music. He would get a funny look on his face and I would say what are you thinking about and he would always be thinking about music.

If we were in a restaurant sometimes Orpheus would look sullen and wouldn't talk to me and I thought people felt sorry for me. I should have realized that women envied me. Their husbands talked too much.

But I wanted to talk to him about my notions. I was working on a new philosophical system. It involved hats.

This is what it is to love an artist: The moon is always rising above your house. The houses of your neighbors look dull and lacking in moonlight. But he is always going away from you. Inside his head there is always something more beautiful.

Orpheus said the mind is a slide ruler. It can fit around anything. Words can mean anything. Show me your body, he said. It only means one thing.

All Aboard the Marriage Hearse
Matt Morillo

Play Synopsis: Sean and Amy are your typical co-habitating, Catholic/Jewish, twentysomething couple living in Manhattan. They work hard, love each other and share common goals in life. Well, sort of. After nearly three years together, Amy wants to get married but Sean does not believe in the institution. Tonight is the night when they will settle the marriage question once and for all.

Character: Amy
Age: 20s – 30s
Genre: Dramatic

Scene Synopsis: Frustrated with the course of their relationship, Amy confronts her boyfriend Matt about her sacrifices, fears, and desires.

Notes:

All Aboard the Marriage Hearse

AMY. I didn't want to move in here into your grandmother's apartment but I did. I wanted you to move in with me in Astoria. But you had to be in Manhattan. I didn't want to lie to your crazy mother about us living together. But I did it. When Patrick's wife caught him drinking again and threw him out, I didn't want him to stay here for three months. But I kept my mouth shut because I knew how close of a friend he was to you.

My point is that when you are in a relationship, you compromise. You do whatever you have to do to make your partner happy. I don't think I'm asking for a lot. All I want is for you to make a promise, a promise that you have already made to me, I want you to make the same promise in front of some other people.

I deserve more. I'm a good person and I've busted my ass to support you and help you have your dreams come true. Who supported you when the *Voice* fired you? I did. Who stroked your pathetic little crushed ego? I did. Who helped you get the job at the *New Yorker*? I did. Who typed all your columns when you broke your hand? I did. And now you've got everything you want. Everything. You've got a job you love, a good salary, a popular column and a book about to be published. I have my teaching job, a great family and you. I have everything I want except one thing. And the person I love more than anyone on the planet is the one person who can give it to me. But he won't.

Smoke and Mirrors
Joseph Goodrich

Play Synopsis: Set in the break room of a quasi-governmental organization, *Smoke and Mirrors* follows Anita and a handful of her co-workers through the course of a seemingly normal day, complete with bad cafeteria food, inept bosses, inappropriate e-mails and blood-stained lab-coats. *Smoke and Mirrors* mingles the comic with the nightmarish, creating a world composed of patriotism and cupcakes, of paranoia and air freshener – a world uncomfortably close to our own.

Character: Anita
Age: 30s
Genre: Dramatic

Scene Synopsis: After some prompting from a friend at work, Anita shares a troubling story about their boss, who may be letting personal feelings affect the way she deals with employees like Anita.

ANITA. If you really want to know, I'll tell you. But you've got to understand that I'm not saying anything about her, okay? I'm not criticizing her personal life, I'm just pointing out how her personal life affects things in Transport.

Diane's got this thing for gay guys. As employees. She loves 'em. If you're gay, you can do no wrong. You're not a threat. I mean, you know what Diane looks like, right? She's not exactly, uhhh...I don't know – name a movie star...The point is, a straight woman, a relatively good-looking straight woman, doesn't have a chance. *(Pause.)* Last Friday, I was showing some of the people in Transport a picture of my son. And everyone's oohing and ahhing over it, because he's really cute if I do say so myself. And I do...And Diane – Diane sees us all looking at it and she comes over and she's like, 'What's the occasion, folks?' And I show her the photograph – big

Smoke and Mirrors

mistake – and she's like, 'Oh! He's so...cute!' You know, like how could he be my son if he's so cute. What she's really saying is, 'You fucking breeder. You fucking heterosexual.' Totally sweet on the surface but totally dismissive underneath. So that's the background...Now this morning I just couldn't get the tallies right. Like I said, I tried it by names, numbers, assignments, everything, and it wouldn't add up. And I know it's important, and I know the trucks are waiting, and I know there's a very limited amount of time in which to get the job done. I understand that. And I did finally get it right and everything's okay. But then Diane calls me over to her cubicle and says she wants to have a little talk with me. I say sure and I go over. And we sit down and she's asking me if anything's wrong, am I feeling all right, am I having any problems...And I say no, which is true. Everything's fine. Pretty much. No major problems. And then she says well, she couldn't help but wonder because I seem to be having trouble lately with getting my work done accurately and on time. Which is so not true! I mean, you know how many people we process every day? It's not unusual to occasionally get – not confused, but temporarily lost...Overwhelmed. Plus, we're short on staff because of the hiring freeze. We're all working really hard trying to get everything done...And then she goes, 'I need to be able to depend on you, Anita. If I can't depend on you I may have to reassign you.' Jesus!...None of what she says is true, but that doesn't matter. I have no say in this at all. She's in charge, and if she wants me out of there she can do it like –

(She snaps her fingers.)

– that. And then I'm screwed. It's on my record, and don't even talk about the pay cut...And none of it has anything to do with my work. It's all because I'm a fucking heterosexual shit-bag breeder. *(Pause.)* I don't have anything against her. I just want to get the job done and make a living. I mean, look at me – I know a little something about discrimination.

THEMES: Discrimination, Marriage

Kickass Plays For Women: Nine
Jane Shepard

Play Synopsis: In *Nine*, two women are held in a life-threatening situation and play mind games to keep one another alive. Held in a cell and chained apart, their only currency is words, and balance of power is everything when a single word becomes the hanging point between life and death.

Character: 1
Age: 30s
Genre: Dramatic

Scene Synopsis: One woman tells the other a story that lifts both of their spirits – a story of salvation and hope and the belief that something simple can come to your rescue when you least expect it.

Notes:

THEMES: HOPE, SURVIVAL, STRENGTH

Kickass Plays For Women: Nine

1. I fell in a pond once, at night, when I was really little, and it was so incredibly dark it was just black, and completely cold, and without breath and I was, really I was drowning, because I could swim a little but in the dark of this tomb you don't know which way is up. You just feel the water moving around you and you could be going down but you don't know. Because you don't know where the surface is. You know? It was bad.

And I was just frozen there, with no air and no hope and no idea which way was up. And then you know what happened?

This silver sliver nicked my eye and it made me turn my head, this little blinding flash, and I looked and it was a moonbeam shining down through to me. Up through the water I saw the light spreading out and shimmering above me on the surface and I, I, I don't know how, I fought toward it, and I struggled up, and went up, and with my last breath of life I came up into the night air.

Isn't that something? I was saved by a moonbeam. I – I was saved. I was saved. By a moonbeam.

THEMES: HOPE, SURVIVAL, STRENGTH

Lobelia Lodge
B.J. Burton

Play Synopsis: On the first weekend of summer, Elsie and her friends meet at their cabin in the woods. As Elsie struggles to repair the dilapidated retreat, the other women become too distracted by their own problems to get involved. One evening the women-only weekend is interrupted by the presence of two mysterious men who emerge from the woods. As old and new wounds resurface, conflicts erupt between the hold of the past and the need to let go. Elsie discovers the fate of the lodge as she discovers the importance of friendship in her life.

Character: Diane
Age: 30s
Genre: Dramatic

Scene Synopsis: Diane confronts Elsie about their past and tries to explain her decision to break away from the summer Lodge they visited throughout their childhood, adolescence and adult lives.

Notes:

THEMES: LOVE, FRIENDSHIP, PREGNANCY

Lobelia Lodge

DIANE. God. I thought your mother told you. I thought everybody knew. Charlie and I got married for the usual reason back then. I was pregnant. We were sort of friends, so we got married. And I felt so bad for you. I knew what you must've been thinking – that I was this mean older girl who had taken away your first true love. But think about this – wasn't it better that a twenty-one year old get pregnant than a sixteen year old?

(After a moment.) I had this terrible miscarriage and was politely informed that I could never have any children. He didn't want to adopt, so we got divorced. Then, of course, I met Richard at work and was stupid enough to marry him, and you know the rest of that story. So, you know why I hate this place so much? Because every time I come up here, I think of how much I hurt you! It reminds me of how stupid I was for thinking that anyone could love me just for being me! And then I think about Aunt Winnie and all the time wasted on this place, and I just hate it! I hate it! I don't care if it burns to the ground or what! I don't care if they bulldoze the whole thing over! I don't care! I don't care!

Sealed for Freshness
Doug Stone

Play Synopsis: Set in 1968, during the heyday of Tupperware parties, hostess Bonnie invites a group of neighbors
over for a party. The guest list: perky, rich Jean, Jean's
cranky and very pregnant sister Sinclair, ditzy-blonde Tracy
Ann, and new neighbor Diane, who's made quite a career
selling Tupperware, but at the expense of her marriage.
The mix of personalities and the number of martinis
consumed lead to a great deal of absurd high jinks plus
revelations of an equal number of secrets and insecurities.

Character: Sinclair
Age: 30s
Genre: Dramatic

Scene Synopsis: Disillusioned and trapped, Sinclair reveals
to her friends far more about her marriage, her fears and
her insecurities than anyone expected.

Notes:

Sealed for Freshness

SINCLAIR. Is this cute to you? Is this some cute little toy to you, huh? Something to play with? Show your friends? Well, not to me. This *(Points to her belly.)* …this is eighteen years of responsibility stretching me out. Eighteen years shackled to a walking anchor…you want to trade your life for this? I'm serious. There is no more Tracy Ann after it's born. You are it's keeper. All this has done is made me uglier. So where's my pay off? Huh? What do I get for trading me in? I wanted more than this. I was creative. I had a mind. *(Tapping on her skull.)* There was something here…something else…something great. *(Pause.)* But no, no…and now… now every time I get pregnant, d'you know what I wanna do, huh? *(Calm and monotone.)* I wanna fall belly first on a rake. Yes, I do. Belly first. I have nightmares about my children all the time. And get this, some of my dreams involve the remote chance that this one *(indicating the baby)* won't live so there's not one more to take care of…

Everything I have in my pathetic little house has been broken by them or my husband. They've taken what I could have been. *(Pause.)* You're lucky, Bonnie. You're lucky that your husband doesn't want to screw you anymore. That's the only way mine knows how to show any emotion at all. He comes home whiskey stinkin' drunk and gets on top of me. Would you like that, Bonnie? Huh? Oh, he'll pay attention to you alright. You could be Mrs. Frankie Benevente, wife of a gas station grease monkey. You can have the grease that's caked under his nails digging around inside you. Huh? Sounds good? *(Pauses/shaking with anger.)* And as a bonus, he leaves his work shirt on while he's screwing you and you get to watch the embroidered name "Frankie" coming at you back and forth and back and forth while he grunts and wheezes like a fuckin' animal! *(Pauses/then sadly.)* And the sad thing – the pathetic moral of the story is that you'll appreciate it, Bonnie, yep because it's the only time he'll ever pay attention to you anyway.

THEMES: MARRIAGE, SEX, PREGNANCY

In the Continuum
Danai Gurira and Nikkole Salter

Play Synopsis: *In the Continuum* puts a human face on the devastating impact of AIDS in Africa and America through the lives of two unforgettably courageous women. Living worlds apart, one in South Central LA and the other in Zimbabwe, each experience a kaleidoscopic weekend of life changing revelations in this story of parallel denials and self-discoveries.

Character: Gail
Age: 30s – 40s
Genre: Dramatic

Scene Synopsis: Gail's son, an young athlete already on the rise, has AIDS and no one knows. When he sleeps with Nia, passing the disease on to her, the young woman confronts the family that has been hiding this secret. Despite Nia's desperate and frightening situation, Gail is only concerned with her son, her son's secret, and their family.

Notes:

In the Continuum

GAIL. You kids don't think. You don't think beyond your own little circle of existence. You think this is a video game? This is life. Real life. You don't get to start over! 'Cause he's just a boy, he's a baby, how is he supposed to know how to – when you all just keep tossin' yourselves at him! Don't give me that look. I see the way you look at him. Salivatin' with dollar signs in your eyes. You probably thought that if you latched onto him you could ride him all the way to the top. You think you the first one to try to lock him down? Ask his agent: he's already had two paternity claims. Sit down. Sit back down! Why should I have told you anything, Nia? This is a private family matter. You should have kept your legs closed. And I warned Darnell about ya'll. I said, "Darnell, baby, stay focused. You can't afford to get caught up." I made sure he played in all the right districts, with all the right coaches, he was seen by the recruiters! Look at his trophies. Look at them! Does this look like AIDS to you? Do you think he would be being recruited if anybody knew? Do you think he would be getting a scholarship? That's right! A scholarship for outstanding athletic achievement – to my son. So, no, nobody knows. It's none of they damn business. You consider what people will think about you if they knew. You think they gon' treat you the same? When you mention it, even the people you thought loved you will have you eatin' outta paper plates. Everybody turns on you; little kids say nasty things to you. Even the people at church! They gon' whisper behind your back; point at you in the pew, sayin', "That's what happens to people who sin with the devil." Think it won't happen. Now, I'm trying to help you, Nia, but you have got to promise me – Is this about money? Huh? Cuz I can get you money, Nia. Give me a couple of hours and I'll get you $5,000. How's that sound? That'll be enough to get you a place, have some money left over to do what you got to do. That's what we'll do: I'll get you $5,000 for now, and we can worry about later, later.

Our Leading Lady
Charles Busch

Play Synopsis: Set in Washington, DC, in 1865, the play is about Laura Keene, the British-born stage actress whose company was performing Tom Taylor's *Our American Cousin* at Ford's Theatre the night Abraham Lincoln was shot and killed by John Wilkes Booth. In classic Charles Busch fashion, *Our Leading Lady* is a backstage comedy in which a presidential assassination is not merely a national tragedy but also a vexing interruption in a powerful woman's quest for fame and glory. Imagine the collision of the Civil War era with *Noises Off*.

Character: Laura
Age: 30s – 40s
Genre: Dramatic

Scene Synopsis: When her troupe of actors comes under suspicion from the man investigating Lincoln's assassination, Laura speaks up to defend them all – insisting on their innocence and imploring for their freedom.

Notes:

Our Leading Lady

LAURA. Last night, I was brought very low. I was forced to see myself as my enemies would see me. Or rather as the young woman I once was. And I saw the world around me as I had not seen it for many years and it was a harsh, threatening place. It's as if I had been cruelly shaken from a very long dream.

And now that I've been awake for a day, I shall go back to sleep. I want to return to my beautiful dream of the theatre. I want to remain always in the dressing room or the wings or above all, the stage; the stage, where for a few hours life is as we wish it were and not unfortunately as it is.

*(The show woman in **LAURA** now takes over. She builds to a dazzling finish.)*

Major, I pray you, release this troupe of strolling players. Do not judge them harshly. They seek only to please. Give them back their gaiety, their easy laughter, their mad exuberance. Give them their liberty. It lies within your power. "The quality of mercy is not strained; / It droppeth as the gentle rain from heaven / Upon the place beneath. It is twice blest; / It blesseth him that gives and him that takes. / 'Tis mightiest in the mightiest; it becomes / The throned monarch better than his crown." Major Hopwood, give them back their lives!

THEMES: Freedom, Art, Pride

Everythings Turning into Beautiul
Seth Zvi Rosenfeld

Play Synopsis: This play with music takes place late one Christmas Eve in lonely New York City, when a couple of down-on-their-luck songwriting partners, hitless, loveless and facing their forties, come together for a night of composing and soul searching. Sam and Brenda don't want to compromise their friendship or their working relationship, but this evening will put their partnership to the test.

Character: Brenda
Age: 40s
Genre: Dramatic

Scene Synopsis: Brenda decides to play her most recently composed song for Sam, but when he asks her what her inspiration was, she begins to panic. She wants to let Sam in, but sometimes opening that door is the scariest thing of all.

Notes:

Everythings Turning into Beautiul

BRENDA. I'm having a panic attack talking about a song I wrote. There's insanity in my family. My mother's out of her mind, my father's completely depressed. I've been in and out of therapy for years and nothing seems to change. I've tried medication and stuff. I don't know. I mean I thought that by this time, I'd have kids and a family and I'm just so pissed that it's not in the cards for me. How'd I get here? That's what I wonder. Did I have a good time the first half of my life? I was so focused on making music and living like a rock star and the fucking scene. Then you try to back your way into some kind of normal life and nothing fits. What is it to have a family? To have kids running around. To go shopping for clothes for them and know what their favorite meals are and to be up on the new toys and cartoons and to be responsible for more than your own pathetic life. What is it to have a decent, healthy relationship that doesn't include cops at your door and finding drugs in your bathroom and…the pain…I know so much about pain, Sam…I can't take any more pain…I really can't. I want something decent but I have no experience of it…I really don't know what decency looks like. Is it what my parents had? I was listening to you talking about wanting to die and I wish I was passionate enough about life to want to die but it's not that for me…I have problems living. Like actually living. Feeling that anything new, anything new…I want something new to happen – Something new – Something brand new, Sam…Something that changes my perspective on being alive. Don't smile Sam. That's what I was thinking about when I wrote that song and you have no idea how deadly serious I am!

THEMES: FAMILY, FEAR, LOVE

I Used to Write on Walls
Bekah Brunstetter

Play Synopsis: Diane, Georgia and Joanne are 3 modern women living very different lives. Unbeknownst to them, they are all pining after the same young man, Trevor: sexy, stoned, oblivious; a surfer on a rad, rad philosophical journey. When a beautiful 11 year old girl and Mona (a sexy, widowed astronaut) are thrown into the crosswinds of diverse romantic affairs, hearts will be broken, loves will be lost, and youthful cries of hope, anger, and sadness will be written on walls.

Character: Mother
Age: 50s
Genre: Dramatic

Scene Synopsis: Diane tells her Mother she wants to get married. Worried that her daughter will get hurt again, but trying to understand and relate to her at the same time, Mother reveals a desire from her past, and one of the compromises she made in life.

Notes:

THEMES: DESIRE, LONGING, LOVE

I Used to Write on Walls

MOTHER. No, I do, I get it.

I used to want to make love to a musician. So that I could go watch him make his music, in some remotely crowded place, and I could sit in a corner and watch him and think, I make love to that person. That body is mine.

That's all I ever wanted. But none of them ever wanted me. They like girls who can use their hair as blankets and women who were raped as children.

Why is it whenever you want one thing you end up with the exact opposite? What sort of fate is that?

Well I pushed this aside. I pushed it way deep down in, forgot it. But it was about ten years ago when I saw a dirty man on the street with a guitar and I looked at him and I loved him and I stood and watched.

I gave him fifty dollars for his guitar. He only asked for twenty. He was hungry and he had a kitten on a string that needed to eat.

I took the guitar home to your father, I said here. I said, learn to play this, or I might accidentally no longer love you. He took it in his hands. It was foreign, but I said, pretend it's a gun.

It was the best five minutes of my life.

Because just for a moment, what I had and what I wanted were the same thing.

Rose Colored Glass
Susan Bigelow and Janice Goldberg

Play Synopsis: Set in 1938 Chicago, *Rose Colored Glass* takes place in the back rooms of Lady O'Riley's and Rose Fleishman's delicatessen. Their disparate worlds are about to collide. In a series of stunning flashbacks, the moving story of how Lady and Rose formed a united front to bring Rose's nephew out of Europe before the war is revealed. This unique work shows the beginning of the holocaust from our side of the ocean and how two remarkable women struggle with American apathy and their own prejudices.

Character: Lady
Age: 50s – 60s
Genre: Dramatic

Scene Synopsis: Lady's son, Tommy left his daughter with Lady and took off. Years later, bearing the weight of his absence and so much more, Lady speaks to a postcard Tommy recently sent, finally letting out a little of her pain and worry.

Notes:

Rose Colored Glass

LADY. Oh, Tommy! *(Looking at the card.)* Why does God keep punishing me for letting you go? Iowa! It's not my fault you had wanderin' feet like your father. It's not my fault Paddy couldn't hear ya' when ya' tried to tell him so...

> *(**LADY** moves into her kitchen, grabs a bottle of whiskey off the shelf, pours a shot, drinks it, and holds the letter.)*

Tommy, I got a pub to run and I'm pourin' beer and feeding everyone in the neighborhood as fast as I can, and every time I turn around Father Patrick's asking me to serve at the soup kitchen, and then the Catholic ladies are always wanting cookies for another one of their bazaars... And now I got the poor Jewish lady borrowing sugar and screamin' about Europe...and, on top of all of that, I have your 13-year-old daughter... I let you go because you said it was killin' you to stay. Well, it killed Paddy when you left. God, I'm an old woman. When is enough enough???

THEMES: Consequences, Death, Family

Oldest Living Confederate Widow: Her Confession

Allan Gurganus and Jane Holding

Play Synopsis: Lucy Marsden, 99 years old, scares and charms us as the widow of the American Civil War's last surviving soldier. His child bride and the mother of his nine children, she now lives on alone, the survivor of the survivor. A born storyteller, a woman of passion and compassion, she finally confesses her own marriage as the secret history of War itself. The role of Lucy – funny, irreverent, candid and heartfelt – offers the actress of any age a sampler for her every emotion and available skill.

Character: Lucille
Age: 50s -90s (99 in the text)
Genre: Dramatic

Scene Synopsis: Lucille reminisces about domestic life, how some habits die hard, and what comfort routine can bring to a person.

Notes:

Oldest Living Confederate Widow:
Her Confession

LUCILLE. I love boiling my own water.

Used to be, a stove was mostly where you'd find me.

First thing all day, I'd turn toward water, the comfort of boiling each morning's worth. Back then, from Child #1 through 8 then 9, I'd be the first awake, naturally. Right off, I'd stack kindling in my Wedgwood stove. From the pump, I'd fill one favorite white enamel saucepan rimmed with red. Oh, to be up and puttering in a big still-sleeping house, to hear the paperboy lob today's "Falls' Herald Traveler" onto, more or less, our front porch, to hear his bike click off, followed by the toenails of his dog on Summit Avenue's bricks. From the window over my sink, our backyard looked to be a dresser drawer full of mist.

I was never one to use a kettle. (Teapot whistles make me nervous). No, I liked to see my water boil. I like to smell my water, feel its steam uncurl. At this early hour, water offered me my best company, felt too perfect to be local, was more a spirit friend.

My morning mood I gauged by water's speed in boiling. If it happened quick, I felt more 'up'. If it took forever, was going to be one of them days.

I was often tired. That I know. Looking back, you don't want to misremember nor soften one little thing. That'd be wrong. I'd ruther sound too harsh. And yet, I admit, at times and from this distance, mis-recalling sure is tempting. Especially about our house before the others rose. The wall beneath our Seth Thomas clock was penciled with their changing heights. I recall my own home kitchen as being so huge – half a train depot full of eastern light. And with my water boiling, my heart to heart with morning.

You know what water is? Water's family.

Barrio Hollywood
Elaine Romero

Play Synopsis: A young Mexican-American boxer dreams of fighting his way out of his family's economic plight. His sister dreams of owning her own dance studio. Their flamboyant mother dreams of taking her poker winnings and going on an extended vacation to the Canary Islands. The family's dreams are deferred when the young boxer sustains a brutal head injury in the boxing ring. As her brother's condition worsens, the dancer and her family learn how far they are willing to go in the name of love. **Published in English and Spanish.**

Character: Amá
Age: 50s – 60's
Genre: Dramatic

Scene Synopsis: Amá's son, who was on life support, has died – and an investigation surrounding his death has begun. Someone killed him, and Amá – distrustful of Alex, the white doctor her daughter has fallen in love with – knows just where to place the blame.

Notes:

AMÁ. My son. My child is dead. And you blame me? He killed him. Michael took Alex's throat in his hands and he killed him. I saw the whole thing. That horrible man murdered my son. I *am* a witness! I want that man to go to the electric chair! I want him dead! Let him feel what it feels like to be murdered. *(More upset.)* My son was going to be fine. He had a difficult few months, but he was going to be fine. *(Short beat.)* I did not sneak off. I went out for some air. *(Short beat.)* No, I did not know he was dead when I left. I had no idea until you said it to me. What do you mean – contradicting myself?

Barrio Hollywood

(Beat.) You already have ideas in your head. I can see them floating around in there. I can see that! I didn't go to school. I don't have perfect English like you, but I can see this. This is not right. *(Short beat.)* I saw everything. Don't pretend. When you know. *(Breaking down.)* The truth. Let me see Graciela. She knows why this happened. *(To herself)* Taking me from my church. From my prayers. When my God comforts me. That's who I love. That's who I listen to. *El siempre está conmigo.* You and your fancy cars. You and your guns. You've never done nothing good for me. *(Short beat; yelling to someone as if he's leaving)* Give me back my suitcase! My son gave me that. *Para mi cumpleaños.* For my birthday trip. He's giving it to me as a gift. When Graciela turns thirty, I turn fortyeight. Only two days apart. *(Getting emotional.)* I saw that pretty island on Channel 52. I saw it in *Espanich.* It was a beautiful place with canaries up in the trees. And water – bluer than your eyes. You can see little canaries there like lizards in the desert. Singing all the time. Making everybody happy. And everybody could be happy if some people let God do His job.

(Amá starts crying.)

Simple things. That's all I ever wanted. *(Short beat.)* I didn't kill Alex with my hands but by wanting so much. And he wanted so much to give me those things. He fought when he was bleeding. When he couldn't see. He fought for money. But I kept wanting more. And you know how God feels about that! You must accept what He gives you. And smile. BECAUSE THAT IS HOW GOD WORKS! He makes the rules. He decides. And you take it. Whatever hand you're dealt. But you gotta keep your poker face on. You gotta look like you're winning or you lose that much more. My grandfather taught me that. He was a poker player from Chihuahua. He knew how to fool people into believing him. *(Quickly.)* That's not what I meant.

AUTHOR INDEX

THEMATIC INDEX

OTHER MONOLOGUE COLLECTIONS AVAILABLE FROM SAMUEL FRENCH

All's Well That Ends Swell
50 Fabulous Classical Monologues for Men
50 Fabulous Classical Monologues for Women
Both Sides of the Story
Next!
His & Hers
Actors Write for Actors
Going Solo
Listen to This
Encore!
Two Minutes to Shine, Volumes 1-5

෴

SAMUELFRENCH.COM

CPSIA information can be obtained at www.ICGtesting.com
Printed in the USA
BVOW011117170612

292888BV00006B/9/P